Tunisian Crochet
for Baby

Sharon Hernes Silverman

Photography by Alan Wycheck and Tiffany Blackstone

STACKPOLE
BOOKS

Published by
STACKPOLE BOOKS
5067 Ritter Road
Mechanicsburg, PA 17055
www.stackpolebooks.com

Printed in the United States of America

10 9 8 7 6 5 4 3 2 1

First edition

Cover design by Caroline Stover

Crochet charts created electronically by Ron Carboni

Cover photograph and photographs on pages 18, 22, 27, 31, and 32 by Tiffany
Blackstone

All other photographs by Alan Wycheck

Standard yarn weight system chart, skill level symbols, baby size chart, and head
circumference chart used courtesy of the Craft Yarn Council of America (CYCA),
www.yarnstandards.com.

Library of Congress Cataloging-in-Publication Data

Silverman, Sharon Hernes, author.
    Tunisian crochet for baby / Sharon Hernes Silverman ; photography by Alan
Wycheck and Tiffany Blackstone. — First edition.
      pages cm
    Includes bibliographical references and index.
    ISBN 978-0-8117-1287-3
    1. Crocheting—Tunisia.   2. Crocheting—Patterns.   3. Infants' clothing.
I. Title.
TT819.T8S55   2014
746.43'4—dc23
                                2014014849

Contents

Introduction   iv

Projects   1

Checkerboard Blanket   2
Checkerboard Hat   6
Honeycomb Pullover   10
Sherbet Stripes Blanket   18
Sherbet Stripes Hat   22
Infant Cocoon and Hat   27
Christening Gown, Bonnet, and Booties   34
Strappy Pants   53
Sunny Bow Headband   58
Nursery Box   62
Washcloth Quartet   65
Harlequin Blanket   73
Thumbless Mittens   79
Zippered Hoodie   82
Favorite Skirt   97
Spring Poncho and Turban   101

Techniques   107

Traditional Crochet Skills Refresher   108
Tunisian Crochet Skills Refresher   113
Beyond the Basics   123

Abbreviations   133
Resources   134
Acknowledgments   138
Visual Index   139

Introduction

Welcome to *Tunisian Crochet for Baby*! Whether you are making a gift or getting ready for a precious bundle of your own, this book gives you a variety of adorable projects—from quick and easy hats to cozy sweaters—to choose from.

This book is intended for people who are already comfortable with basic crochet stitches (chain, single crochet, and double crochet). Before you start the projects, review basic crochet instructions in the back of the book if you need to.

Tunisian crochet allows you to use your crochet hook to create fabrics that look knitted or woven. All of the basics are explained in the back of the book. (If you are new to Tunisian crochet and want more detailed instructions on how to get started with the technique, you might find my book *Tunisian Crochet: The Look of Knitting with the Ease of Crocheting* helpful.) Instructions for any special stitches or techniques are included in the patterns or in the Techniques section.

Symbol charts are also provided for each pattern. These visual representations are included to help make specific sections of the patterns easy to understand. See page 132 for instructions on how to read charts.

Reference materials, including information on yarn and hook suppliers, a yarn weight chart, and sizing charts, appear at the end of the book.

I hope that the patterns inspire you to make Tunisian crochet projects for the babies in your life. Happy crocheting!

Projects

Checkerboard Blanket

SKILL LEVEL

INTERMEDIATE

This pattern combines Tunisian double crochet post stitch and Tunisian simple stitch. Even though the finished item has a checkerboard effect, each row uses only one color. It's easier than it looks!

MEASUREMENTS

34 in. (86.5 cm) square

MATERIALS

Lion Brand Yarn Cotton-Ease (50% cotton, 50% acrylic; 3.5 oz./100 g; 207 yd./188 m)

Medium

Color A: Almond (099), 4 skeins

Color B: Hazelnut (125), 4 skeins

U.S. size J-10 (6 mm) Tunisian crochet hook (or size needed to obtain gauge)

Tapestry needle

GAUGE

15 sts and 15 rows in pattern = 4 in. (10.2 cm), blocked

Special Stitch

Tunisian Front Post Double Crochet (Tfpdc)

Yo, insert hook around both strands of vertical bar or around post, as indicated in pattern, yo, pull up lp, yo, pull through 2 lps—1 lp added to hook.

Notes

1. When changing colors, do not cut yarn unless instructed to do so.

2. For the Tunisian front post double crochet stitches in this pattern, you'll be working around both strands of the next stitch two rows below (or around the post of a Tfpdc stitch two rows below). The hook remains at the front of the work.

3. See page 130 for step-by-step photos and instructions for working Tunisian front post double crochet.

The first Tfpdcs will be worked into the stitch 2 rows below.

Tfpdcs in following rows will be worked around the posts of previous Tfpdcs.

Pattern

With A, ch 120.

Row 1: Tss in second ch from hook and in each ch across—120 lps on hook. Return.

Row 2: Sk first vertical bar. *Tss in next st. Repeat from * across—120 lps on hook. Return, changing to B when 2 lps remain on hook.

Row 3: Sk first vertical bar. Tfpdc around both strands of next vertical bar of Row 1. *Tss in each of next 2 vertical bars of Row 2, Tfpdc around both strands of next vertical bar of Row 1. Repeat from * across to final st. Tss in final st—120 lps on hook. Return.

Row 4: Sk first vertical bar. *Tss in next st. Repeat from * across—120 lps on hook. Return, changing to A when 2 lps remain on hook.

Section of Pattern

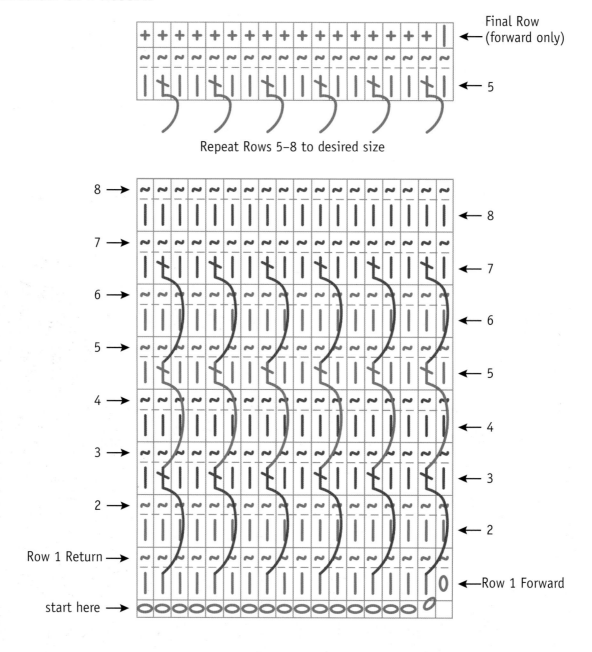

Final Row (forward only) ← Final Row

← 5

Repeat Rows 5–8 to desired size

8 →   ← 8

7 →   ← 7

6 →   ← 6

5 →   ← 5

4 →   ← 4

3 →   ← 3

2 →   ← 2

Row 1 Return →   ← Row 1 Forward

start here →

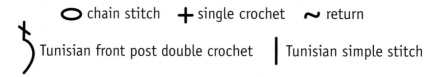

O chain stitch **+** single crochet **~** return

Tunisian front post double crochet **|** Tunisian simple stitch

Row 5: Sk first vertical bar. Tfpdc around post of first Tfpdc two rows below. *Tss in each of next 2 vertical bars. Tfpdc around post of next Tfpdc two rows below. Repeat from * across to final st. Tss in final st—120 lps on hook. Return.

Row 6: Repeat Row 4, changing to B when 2 lps remain on hook.

Row 7: Sk first vertical bar. Tfpdc around post of first Tfpdc two rows below. *Tss in each of next 2 vertical bars, Tfpdc around post of next Tfpdc two rows below. Repeat from * across to final st. Tss in final st—120 lps on hook. Return.

Row 8: Repeat Row 4, changing to A when 2 lps remain on hook.

Repeat Rows 5–8, working 2 rows in each color, until blanket measures approximately 35.5 in. (90 cm). Cut B after final repeat of Row 8.

Next Row: Repeat Row 5.

Final Row: Sk first vertical bar. Sc in each stitch across, inserting hook in each st as for Tss—119 sc.

Fasten off.

Finishing

With tapestry needle, weave in ends. Lightly steam block on WS.

Checkerboard Hat

SKILL LEVEL

■■■□

INTERMEDIATE

This pattern, a companion to the Checkerboard Blanket, combines Tunisian double crochet post stitch and Tunisian simple stitch. Pom-poms in the corners make it irresistibly adorable!

MEASUREMENTS

14.5 in. (37 cm) around; 7 in. (18 cm) from brim to crown

MATERIALS

Lion Brand Yarn Cotton-Ease (50% cotton, 50% acrylic; 3.5 oz./100 g; 207 yd./188 m)

Medium

Color A: Almond (099), 1 skein

Color B: Hazelnut (125), 1 skein

NOTE: If you are also making the Checkerboard Blanket, you will have enough yarn left over from the blanket to complete the hat.

U.S. size K-10½ (6.5 mm) Tunisian crochet hook

Tapestry needle

GAUGE

14 sts and 13 rows in pattern = 4 in. (10.2 cm), blocked

Special Stitch

Tunisian Front Post Double Crochet (Tfpdc)

Yo, insert hook around both strands of vertical bar or around post, as indicated in pattern, yo, pull up lp, yo, pull through 2 lps—1 lp added to hook.

Note

See page 130 for step-by-step photos and instructions for working Tunisian front post double crochet.

Pattern

With A, ch 48.

Row 1: Tps in second ch from hook and in next ch, *Tks in next 2 chs, Tps in next 2 chs. Repeat from * across until 1 st remains, Tks in final ch—48 lps on hook. Return.

Row 2: Sk first vertical bar. *Tps in next 2 sts, Tks in next 2 sts. Repeat from * across until 3 sts remain. Tps in next 2 sts, Tks in final st—48 lps on hook. Return.

Rows 3–4: Repeat Row 2. Change to B at end of Row 4 return when 2 lps remain on hook. Do not cut A.

Row 5: Sk first vertical bar. *Tss in next st. Repeat from * across—48 lps on hook. Return.

Row 6: Repeat Row 5, changing to A when 2 lps remain on hook. Do not cut B.

Row 7: Sk first vertical bar. Tfpdc around both strands of next vertical bar two rows below. *Tss in each of next 2 vertical bars, Tfpdc around both strands of next vertical bar two rows below. Repeat from * across until 1 st remains. Tss in final st—48 lps on hook. Return.

Row 8: Sk first vertical bar. *Tss in next st. Repeat from * across—48 lps on hook. Return, changing to B when 2 lps remain on hook.

Row 9: Sk first vertical bar. Tfpdc around post of first Tfpdc two rows below. *Tss in each of next 2 vertical bars, Tfpdc around post of next Tfpdc two rows below. Repeat from * across to final st. Tss in final st—48 lps on hook. Return.

Row 10: Repeat Row 8, changing to A when 2 lps remain on hook.

Rows 11–20: Repeat Rows 9–10, continuing to change colors every 2 rows. Cut A after changing to B at end of Row 20.

Row 21: Repeat Row 9.

Row 22: Sk first vertical bar. Sc in each st across, inserting hook in each st as for Tss—47 sc. Fasten off.

Assembly

Turn hat inside out. Using tapestry needle, sew back seam. Lightly steam block, making sure seam is at center back of piece.

Turn hat right side out. With A, whipstitch top seam closed. The stitching is meant to show. (If you prefer not to see the whipstitching, use color B instead.)

Weave in ends.

Pom-Pom (make 2)

1. Cut two circles of cardboard approximately 3.75 in. (9.5 cm) in diameter. Find the center of each circle. Cut a smaller hole, approximately 1 in. (2.5 cm) in diameter, in the center of each cardboard circle to form rings. Cut through the ring on one side so you can slide the yarn into the center hole.

2. Hold the two cardboard rings together and wind the yarn (A and B held together) around both rings at once. Don't wrap too tightly or you will not be able to separate the circles. Continue until the rings are

Hat

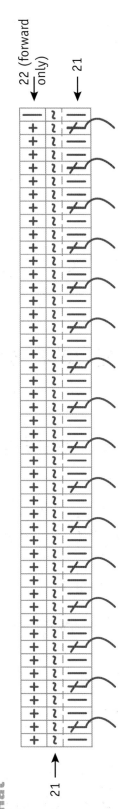

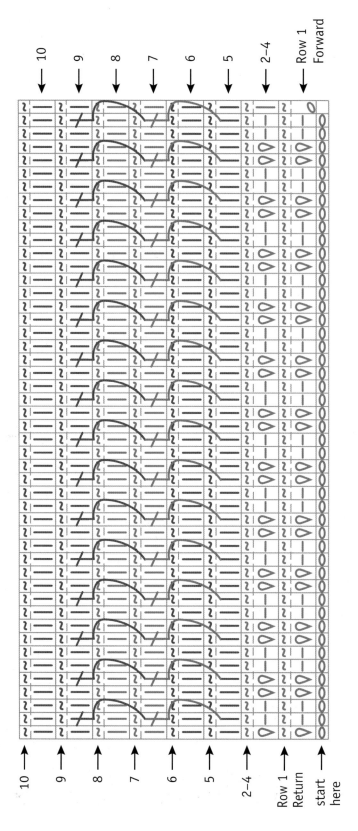

Rows 11–20: continue in pattern, working 2 rows in A, then 2 rows in B, ending with 2 rows in A

φ chain stitch $+$ single crochet $-$ Tunisian simple stitch $\wr$ return

$\mid$ Tunisian front post double crochet $\mid$ Tunisian simple stitch φ Tunisian knit stitch

$-$ Tunisian purl stitch

completely covered; make it nice and thick, with at least 80 wraps.

3. Cut around the outside edge of the yarn wraps, between the two rings. Make sure all the strands of yarn are cut.

4. Cut a length of A approximately 20 in. (50 cm) long. Separate the two cardboard rings slightly. Slip the length of yarn between the rings. Tie into a tight knot. Pull the cardboard gently away. Fluff the pom-pom into a round ball. Trim the pom-pom as desired. Leave the tails of the central tie long, to use for attaching the pom-pom to the hat.

Finishing

Position a pom-pom on a top corner of the hat. Pull the long tie-off tails through to the inside of the hat, a few stitches away from each other. Tie them securely on the inside of the hat, so the pom-pom does not wobble. Weave in the ends. Repeat with the other pom-pom.

Honeycomb Pullover

This sweater is worked with two strands—one solid, one variegated—held together in the alternating Tunisian simple and purl stitches that create the honeycomb stitch.

MEASUREMENTS

Instructions are for size 6 months, with sizes 9 months and 12 months in parentheses.

MATERIALS

Filatura di Crosa Zarina (100% Extra Fine Merino Superwash; 1.75 oz./50 g; 180 yd./165 m)

Fine

Color A: Light yellow (1651), 2 (3, 3) balls

Filatura di Crosa Baby Zarina Print (100% Extra Fine Merino Superwash; 1.75 oz./50 g; 180 yd./165 m)

Color B: White pastel (5086), 2 (3, 3) balls

U.S. size H-8 (5.0 mm) Tunisian crochet hook (or size needed to obtain gauge)

U.S. size G-6 (4.0 mm) regular crochet hook (or size needed to keep neckline trim flat)

Tapestry needle

GAUGE

20 sts and 14 rows with Tunisian hook in pattern and 1 strand each of A and B held together = 4 in. (10.2 cm), blocked

Special Stitch

Crochet cast-on (CCO): *First CCO:* Bring yarn behind hook. Insert a regular crochet hook from left to right in final st and under the Tunisian hook, yo, pull lp through. Move regular crochet hook to top of Tunisian hook, yo, pull lp through. *Subsequent CCOs:* Move yarn toward you then under and behind hook. Bring regular crochet hook in front of and on top of Tunisian hook. Yo, pull lp through. *Final CCO:* Slip last lp from regular crochet hook back onto Tunisian hook. Rotate Tunisian hook back into normal position and commence return pass.

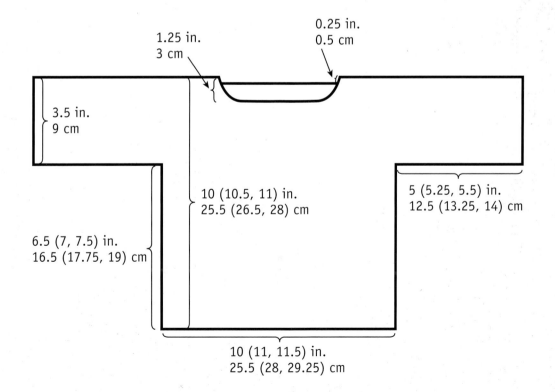

1.25 in.
3 cm

0.25 in.
0.5 cm

3.5 in.
9 cm

10 (10.5, 11) in.
25.5 (26.5, 28) cm

5 (5.25, 5.5) in.
12.5 (13.25, 14) cm

6.5 (7, 7.5) in.
16.5 (17.75, 19) cm

10 (11, 11.5) in.
25.5 (28, 29.25) cm

Sweater Back

For Sweater Front, work through Row 30 (32, 32)

Rows 27–37 (29–39, 31–41): repeat Rows 3 and 2, ending with Row 3

sweater body

ch 26 (28, 30)

26
(28, 30)
25
(27, 29)

CCO 26 (28, 30)

Repeat Rows 2 and 3 through Row 24 (26, 28)

26
(28, 30)
25
(27, 29)

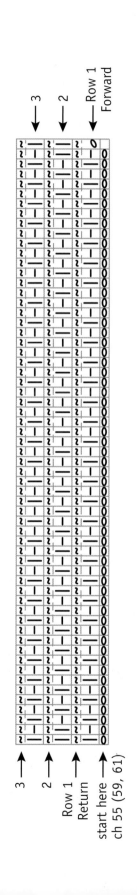

3

2

Row 1
Forward

3

2

Row 1
Return

start here
ch 55 (59, 61)

$\bigcirc$ chain stitch $\underline{}$ Tunisian purl stitch $|$ Tunisian simple stitch $\diagup\!\!\!\!\bigcirc$ crochet cast-on $\wr$ return

Notes

1. Sweater is worked with two strands of yarn held together throughout (one strand of A and one of B).
2. Tunisian honeycomb stitch alternates Tps and Tss. On each row, you will work Tss into Tps from the previous row, and Tps into Tss from the previous row.
3. See page 123 for step-by-step photos and instructions for crochet cast-on.

Pattern

Back

With one strand A and one strand B held together, using Tunisian hook, ch 55 (59, 61).

Row 1 (RS): Tps in second ch from hook, *Tss in next ch, Tps in next ch. Repeat from * across until 1 ch remains, Tss in final ch—55 (59, 61) lps on hook. Return.

Row 2: Sk first vertical bar. *Tss in next st, Tps in next st. Repeat from * across until 2 sts remain. Tss into each of final 2 sts—55 (59, 61) lps on hook. Return.

Row 3: Sk first vertical bar. *Tps in next st, Tss in next st. Repeat from * across. Return.

Rows 4–24 (26, 28): Repeat Rows 2–3, ending with a Row 2.

SLEEVES

Row 25 (27, 29): Ch 26 (28, 30). Tps in second ch from hook. *Tss in next ch, Tps in next ch. Repeat from * across chs, then continue to work in pattern across back (including first vertical bar) to final st. At the end of the back (81 [87, 91] lps on hook), CCO 26 (28, 30) sts—107 (115, 121) lps on hook. Return.

Row 26 (28, 30): Repeat Row 2—107 (115, 121) lps on hook.

Row 27 (29, 31): Repeat Row 3.

Rows 28–37 (30–39, 32–41): Repeat Rows 2–3.

RIGHT BACK NECKLINE SHAPING

Row 38 (40, 42): Work as for Row 2 until there are 40 (44, 46) lps on hook. Leave remaining sts unworked. **Return:** *Yo, pull through 2 lps. Repeat from * until 1 lp remains on hook.

NOTE The return pass of this row differs from standard returns.

Back Neckline Shaping

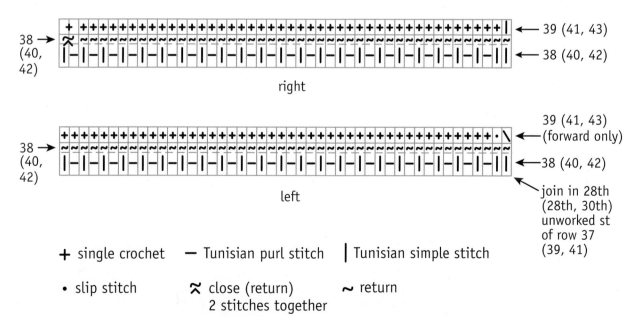

38 (40, 42) → right ← 39 (41, 43) ← 38 (40, 42)

38 (40, 42) → left 39 (41, 43) (forward only) ← 38 (40, 42) join in 28th (28th, 30th) unworked st of row 37 (39, 41)

+ single crochet   **—** Tunisian purl stitch   **|** Tunisian simple stitch

• slip stitch   **≈** close (return) 2 stitches together   **~** return

Row 39 (41, 43): Sk first vertical bar. *Sc in next st, inserting hook as for Tps; sc in next st, inserting hook as for Tss. Repeat from * across right side of sleeve and neck until you have completed 38 (42, 44) sc. Fasten off.

LEFT BACK NECKLINE SHAPING

Row 38 (40, 42): Skip first 27 (27, 29) sts. Rejoin yarn. Work in pattern across to cuff—40 (44, 46) lps on hook. Return.

Row 39 (41, 43): Sk first vertical bar. Sl st in next vertical bar. Sc across, entering each st to keep in pattern—38 (42, 44) sc. Fasten off.

Front

Work as for back through Row 30 (32, 32).

LEFT FRONT NECKLINE SHAPING (WILL BE RIGHT-HAND SIDE OF WORK AS YOU LOOK AT IT)

Row 31 (33, 33): Work in pattern as for Row 3 until there are 42 (46, 48) lps on hook. Leave remaining sts unworked.

Return: *Yo, pull through 2 lps. Repeat from * until 1 lp remains on hook.

NOTE The return pass of this row differs from the standard return.

Row 32 (34, 34): Work in pattern as for Row 2 until there are 41 (45, 47) lps on the hook. **Return:** Work as for Row 31 (33, 33) return.

Row 33 (35, 35): Work in pattern as for Row 3 until there are 40 (44, 46) lps on the hook. **Return:** Work as for Row 31 (33, 33) return.

Left Front Neckline Shaping

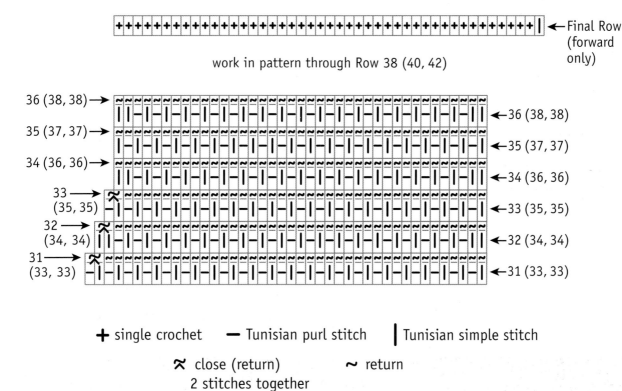

← Final Row
(forward only)

work in pattern through Row 38 (40, 42)

+ single crochet   **—** Tunisian purl stitch   **|** Tunisian simple stitch

≿ close (return)
2 stitches together

∼ return

Rows 34–38 (36–40, 36–42): Work in pattern as for Rows 2 and 3 until there are 39 (43, 45) lps on the hook. Return (standard return).

Row 39 (41, 43): Sk first vertical bar. Insert hook in next st to remain in pattern, yo, pull up lp, yo, pull through 2 lps (sc made). Continue across, entering each st to remain in pattern until you have completed 38 (42, 44) sc. Fasten off.

RIGHT FRONT NECKLINE SHAPING (WILL BE LEFT-HAND SIDE OF WORK AS YOU LOOK AT IT)

Row 31 (33, 33): Leave 23 (23, 25) sts unworked. Rejoin yarn. Work in pattern across to cuff—42 (46, 48) lps on hook. Return.

Row 32 (34, 34): Sk first vertical bar. Sl st in next st. Work in pattern across—41 (45, 47) lps on hook. Return.

Row 33 (35, 35): Sk first vertical bar. Sl st in next st. Work in pattern across—40 (44, 46) lps on hook. Return.

Row 34 (36, 36): Sk first vertical bar. Sl st in next st. Work in pattern across—39 (43, 45) lps on hook. Return.

Rows 35–38 (37–40, 37–42): Sk first vertical bar. Work in pattern across—39 (43, 45) lps on hook. Return.

Row 39 (41, 43): Sk first vertical bar. Insert hook in next st to remain in pattern, yo, pull up lp, yo, pull through 2 lps (sc made). Continue across, entering each st to remain in pattern until you have completed 38 (42, 44) sc. Fasten off.

Right Front Neckline Shaping

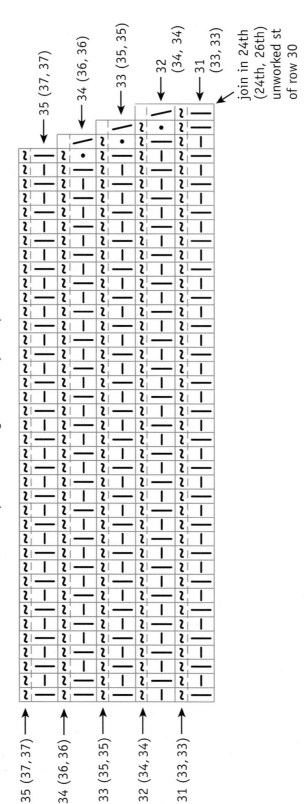

Final Row

35 (37, 37)

34 (36, 36)

33 (35, 35)

32 (34, 34)

31 (33, 33)

join in 24th (24th, 26th) unworked st of row 30

work in pattern through Row 38 (40, 42)

35 (37, 37) →

34 (36, 36) →

33 (35, 35) →

32 (34, 34) →

31 (33, 33) →

+ single crochet   **—** Tunisian purl stitch   **❘** Tunisian simple stitch   **•** slip stitch   **ↄ** return

Neckline Trim

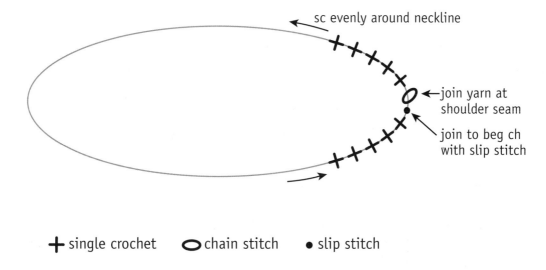

sc evenly around neckline

←join yarn at
shoulder seam

join to beg ch
with slip stitch

✛ single crochet ⬭ chain stitch • slip stitch

Assembly

Using tapestry needle, weave in ends. Lightly steam block pieces on WS. Using one strand of solid-color yarn, sew shoulder, underarm, and side seams. Block seams flat.

Neckline Trim

Turn sweater right side out. With B and regular crochet hook, join yarn at either shoulder seam. Ch 1. Sc in each st around neck opening, entering all of the Tunisian sts as for Tss, and working in the ends of the neckline decrease rows. Join to beg ch with sl st. Fasten off. Weave in ends.

Sherbet Stripes Blanket

SKILL LEVEL

EASY

Luscious colors make this blanket a standout. The striped main section, worked in Tunisian simple stitch, is trimmed with shell edging in regular crochet.

MEASUREMENTS

31.5 in. (80 cm) by 33 in. (84 cm)

MATERIALS

Plymouth Yarn Encore (75% acrylic, 25% wool;
3.5 oz./100 g, 200 yd./183 m)

Medium

Color A: Yellow (215), 2 skeins

Color B: Carnation (457), 2 skeins

Color C: Pink (449), 2 skeins

U.S. size H-8 (5.0 mm) Tunisian crochet hook
(or size needed to obtain gauge)

U.S. size G-6 (4.0 mm) regular crochet hook

Tapestry needle

GAUGE

Gauge is flexible for this project. Suggested gauge:
18 stitches and 12 rows in Tss = 4 in. (10.2 cm),
blocked

Note

Do not cut yarn unless instructed to do so. Let it hang
to the back and pick it up the next time the pattern
calls for it.

Section of Pattern

← 107
(forward
only)

Rows 86–106: repeat Rows 2–22
Rows 44–85: repeat Rows 2–43
Rows 26–43: repeat Rows 23–25 six times

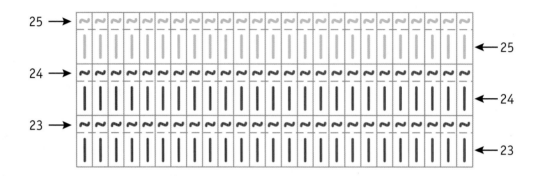

Rows 5–22: repeat Rows 2–4 six times

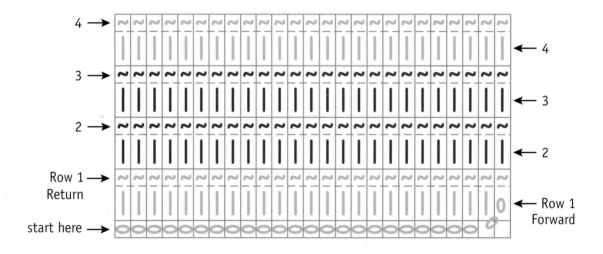

O chain stitch   **|** Tunisian simple stitch   **+** single crochet   **~** return   **•** slip stitch

Trim

| double crochet | + single crochet | • slip stitch | ◯ chain stitch | ↑ turn |

Pattern

With A and Tunisian crochet hook, ch 129.

Row 1 (RS): Tss in second ch from hook and each ch across—129 lps on hook. Return.

Row 2: With B, sk first vertical bar. *Tss in each st across. Return.

Row 3: Repeat Row 2, changing to A when 2 lps remain at end of the return.

Row 4: With A, repeat Row 2, changing to B when 2 lps remain at end of the return.

Rows 5–22: Repeat Rows 2–4 six times. Change to C when 2 lps remain at the end of Row 22 return. Cut B, leaving at least a 4-inch tail.

Rows 23–24: With C, repeat Row 2, changing to A when 2 lps remain at the end of Row 24 return.

Row 25: With A, repeat Row 2, changing to C when 2 lps remain at the end of the return.

Rows 26–43: Repeat Rows 23–25 six times, changing to B when 2 lps remain at the end of Row 43 return. Cut C.

Rows 44–85: Repeat Rows 2–43.

Rows 86–106: Repeat Rows 2–22, but do not change to C at the end of Row 106.

Row 107: Switch to regular crochet hook. Sk first vertical bar. Sc in each st across, inserting hook into each st as for Tss—128 sc. Fasten off.

Finish Main Section

With tapestry needle, weave in ends. Lightly steam block on WS.

Trim

Row 1: With WS facing and using regular crochet hook, join C in any corner. Ch 1. Sc in each st and row end around, working 2 or 3 sc in each corner to keep them square. Join to beg ch with sl st.

> **NOTE** Because the rows of Tunisian crochet are taller than single crochet stitches are wide, work slightly more loosely on the long sides of the blanket (or use a larger crochet hook) if necessary to keep blanket edge even and flat.

Row 2: Ch 1, turn. *Sk 1 sc, 5 dc in next st, sk 1 sc, sc in next sc. Repeat from * around. Join to beg ch with sl st. Fasten off.

Finishing

With tapestry needle, weave in remaining ends. Lightly steam block if desired.

Sherbet Stripes Hat

SKILL LEVEL

EASY

The sunny colors in this hat match the Sherbet Stripes
Blanket. The ribbed brim is worked in a solid color,
with the Tunisian knit stitch crown worked in stripes.
A fluffy pom-pom adds a flourish.

MEASUREMENTS

Newborn: 12 in. (30.5 cm) circumference

Baby: 14 in. (35.5 cm) circumference

MATERIALS

Plymouth Yarn Encore (75% acrylic, 25% wool; 3.5 oz./100 g; 200 yd./183 m)

Medium

Color A: Pink (449), 1 skein

Color B: Yellow (215), 1 skein

Color C: Carnation (457), 1 skein

U.S. size H-8 (5.0 mm) Tunisian crochet hook (or size needed to obtain gauge)

Two circles of cardboard each approximately 3.75 in. in diameter

Tapestry needle

GAUGE

18 sts and 23 rows in Tks = 4 in. (10.2 cm), blocked

Special Stitch

Tunisian knit stitch 2 together (Tks2tog): Insert hook through next 2 sts at same time, with hook ending at back of work as for Tks. Yo, pull up lp—1 st decreased.

Section of Pattern

repeat Rows 12–14 five (six) times

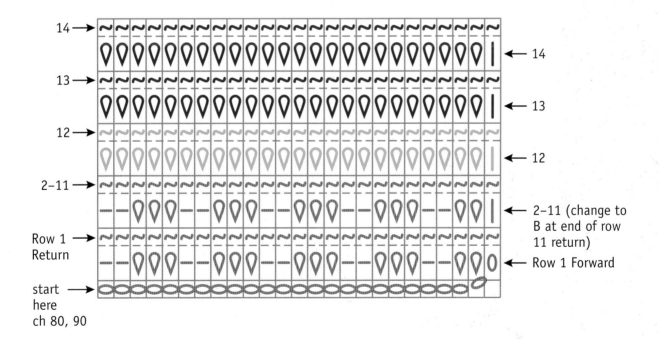

◯ chain stitch   ◊ Tunisian knit stitch   — Tunisian purl stitch   ∼ return

Notes

1. Instructions are written for newborn size. Instructions for baby size are given in parentheses.
2. See page 131 for step-by-step photos and instructions for working Tunisian knit stitch 2 together.

Pattern

With A, ch 80 (90).

Row 1(RS): Tks in second ch from hook and in next ch, Tps in next 2 chs. *Tks in next 3 chs, Tps in next 2 chs. Repeat from * across—80 (90) lps on hook. Return.

Row 2: Sk first vertical bar. Tks in next 2 sts, Tps in next 2 sts. *Tks in next 3 sts, Tps in next 2 sts. Repeat from * across. Return.

Rows 3–11: Repeat Row 2. Change to B when 2 lps remain at the end of Row 11 return. Cut A, leaving a long tail for sewing the folded brim.

Row 12: Sk first vertical bar. Tks in each st across. Return. Change to C when 2 lps remain at end of return.

Rows 13–14: Repeat Row 12, changing to B when 2 lps remain at end of Row 14 return.

Rows 15–29 (15–32): Repeat Rows 12–14 five (six) times. Change to B when 2 lps remain at end of Row 29 (32) return.

Crown Shaping

Row 1: Sk first vertical bar. Tks in next 3 sts, Tks2tog. *Tks in next 4 sts, Tks2tog. Repeat from * across until 2 (0) sts remain, Tks in remaining sts—67 (75) lps on hook. Return, changing to C when 2 lps remain on hook.

Row 2: Sk first vertical bar. *Tks in each st across—67 (75) lps on hook. Return.

Row 3: Sk first vertical bar. Tks in next 2 sts, Tks2tog. *Tks in next 3 sts, Tks2tog. Repeat from * across until 2 (0) sts remain, Tks in remaining sts—54 (60) lps on hook. Return, changing to B when 2 lps remain on hook.

Row 4: Sk first vertical bar. *Tks in each st across—54 (60) lps on hook. Return, changing to C when 2 lps remain on hook.

Row 5: Sk first vertical bar. Tks in next st, Tks2tog. *Tks in next 2 sts, Tks2tog. Repeat from * across until 2 (0) sts remain, Tks in remaining sts—41 (45) lps on hook. Return.

Row 6: Sk first vertical bar. *Tks in each st across—41 (45) lps on hook. Return, changing to B when 2 lps remain on hook.

Row 7: Sk first vertical bar. Tks2tog. *Tks, Tks2tog. Repeat from * across until 2 (0) sts remain, Tks in remaining sts—28 (30) lps on hook. Return, changing to C when 2 lps remain on hook.

Row 8: Sk first vertical bar. Tks in each st across—28 (30) lps on hook. Return.

Row 9: Sk first vertical bar. *Tks2tog. Repeat from * across until 1 (1) st remains, Tks in remaining st—15 (16) lps on hook. Return, changing to B when 2 lps remain on hook.

Row 10: Sk first vertical bar. Tks in each st across—15 (16) lps on hook. Return, changing to C when 2 lps remain on hook.

Row 11: Sk first vertical bar. *Tks2tog. Repeat from * across until 0 (1) sts remain, Tks in remaining st—8 (9) lps on hook. Return.

Newborn Size: Fasten off, leaving a long tail.

Baby Size: Continue with Row 12.

Row 12: Sk first vertical bar. Tks in each st across—9 lps on hook. Return. Fasten off, leaving a long tail.

Finishing and Assembly

Lightly steam block hat on WS.

Fold brim under to the inside of the hat. On the WS of the piece, sew the bottom edge of Row 1 to Row 11, using long tail from end of Row 11.

With WS facing, sew back seam. Sew top of hat closed. Turn right side out.

Weave in ends.

Pom-Pom

1. Cut two circles of cardboard approximately 3.75 in. (9.5 cm) in diameter. Find the center of each circle. Cut a smaller hole, approximately 1 in. (2.5 cm) in diameter, in the center of each cardboard circle to form rings. Cut through the ring on one side so you can slide the yarn into the center hole.

Crown Shaping (Section)

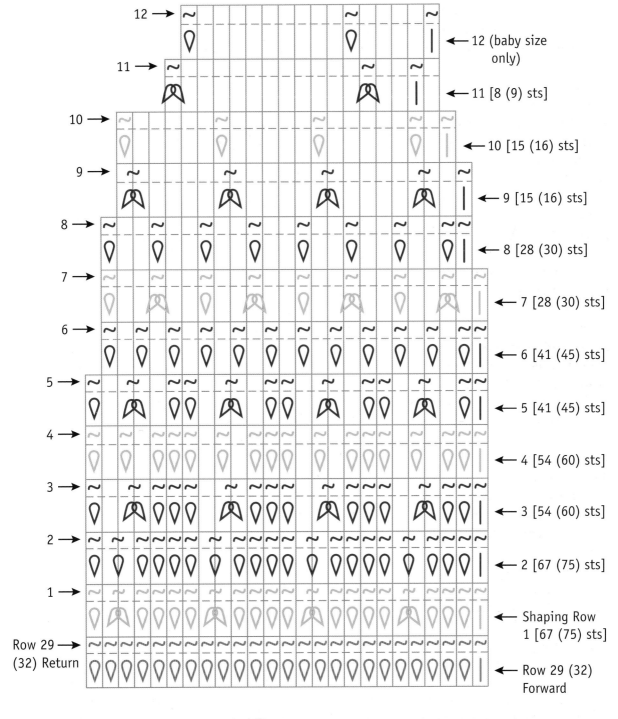

12 →

← 12 (baby size only)

11 →

← 11 [8 (9) sts]

10 →

← 10 [15 (16) sts]

9 →

← 9 [15 (16) sts]

8 →

← 8 [28 (30) sts]

7 →

← 7 [28 (30) sts]

6 →

← 6 [41 (45) sts]

5 →

← 5 [41 (45) sts]

4 →

← 4 [54 (60) sts]

3 →

← 3 [54 (60) sts]

2 →

← 2 [67 (75) sts]

1 →

← Shaping Row 1 [67 (75) sts]

Row 29 (32) Return →

← Row 29 (32) Forward

Tunisian knit stitch   Tunisian knit stitch 2 together   ～ return

2. Hold the two cardboard rings together and wind the yarn (all three colors held together) around both rings at once. Don't wrap too tightly or you will not be able to separate the circles. Continue until the rings are completely covered; make it nice and thick.

3. Cut around the outside edge of the yarn wraps, between the two rings. Make sure all the strands of yarn are cut.

4. Cut a length of C approximately 20 in. (50 cm) long. Separate the two cardboard rings slightly. Slip the length of yarn between the rings. Tie into a tight knot. Pull the cardboard gently away. Fluff the pom-pom into a round ball. Trim the pom-pom as desired. Leave the tails of the central tie long, to use for attaching the pom-pom to the hat.

5. Position the pom-pom on the top of the hat and pull both ends of the tie yarn through to the inside, a few stitches apart. Tie the ends securely together on the inside of the hat so the pom-pom does not wobble. Weave in ends.

Infant Cocoon and Hat

Snuggle your newborn into this cozy cocoon and hat ensemble for a once-in-a-lifetime photo opportunity. The seamless cocoon is worked in the round, while the hat is done in rows and then seamed. Once you get a feel for the novelty yarn, the stitches are easy.

SIZE

One size fits newborns up to 11 pounds

MEASUREMENTS

Cocoon: Length from opening to bottom of sack, 15 in. (38 cm); length of tail before knotting, 8 in. (20 cm); circumference, 16 in. (40.5 cm)

Hat: Circumference, 14 in. (35.5 cm); length from brim to point, 7 in. (18 cm)

Note: The cocoon will stretch to fit a range of sizes.

MATERIALS (FOR BOTH COCOON AND HAT)

Yarn A: Plymouth Yarn Adore (100% nylon; 1.8 oz./ 50 g, 74 yd./68 m)

Super Bulky

Neutrals (1003), 1 ball

Yarn B: Plymouth Select Worsted Merino Superwash (100% superwash fine merino wool; 3.5 oz./ 100 g, 218 yd./200 m)

Medium

Cilantro (17), 1 skein

U.S. size K-10½ (6.5 mm) double-ended Tunisian crochet hook (or size needed to obtain gauge)

Stitch marker

Tapestry needle

Note: Cocoon can be made with either a rigid double-ended hook or a double-ended hook joined by a flexible plastic strand.

GAUGE

With B, 17 sts and 13 rows in Tss = 4 in. (10.2 cm), blocked

Special Stitches

Tunisian simple stitch 2 together (Tss2tog): Insert hook through next 2 sts at same time, with hook remaining at front of work as for Tss. Yo, pull up lp—1 st decreased.

Notes

1. When working with novelty yarn, it takes a little practice to know where to place the stitches. Use your fingers to feel for the "core" yarn under the embellishments. Make a small swatch before starting the project to get familiar with the yarn.

2. The cocoon starts at the open end and works toward the knotted tail. The first two rows are worked back and forth in A. They will be sewn together at the end. Starting with Row 3 (and B), the cocoon is worked in the round; you will need two balls of B to do this.

Cocoon

Divide B into 2 equal balls.

With A and double-ended Tunisian crochet hook, ch 64.

Row 1 (RS): Tss in second ch from hook and in each ch across—64 lps on hook. Return.

Row 2: Sk first vertical bar. *Tss in next st. Repeat from * across—64 lps on hook. Return, changing to B when 2 lps remain on hook. Cut A, leaving a 4-inch tail.

Round 3: Sk first vertical bar. Tss in next 31 sts. Rotate project 180 degrees. Slide stitches to other end of hook. You will be looking at the WS of the work.

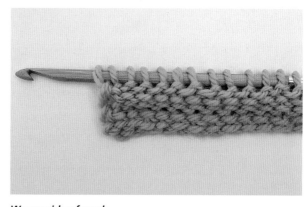

Wrong side of work

Cocoon

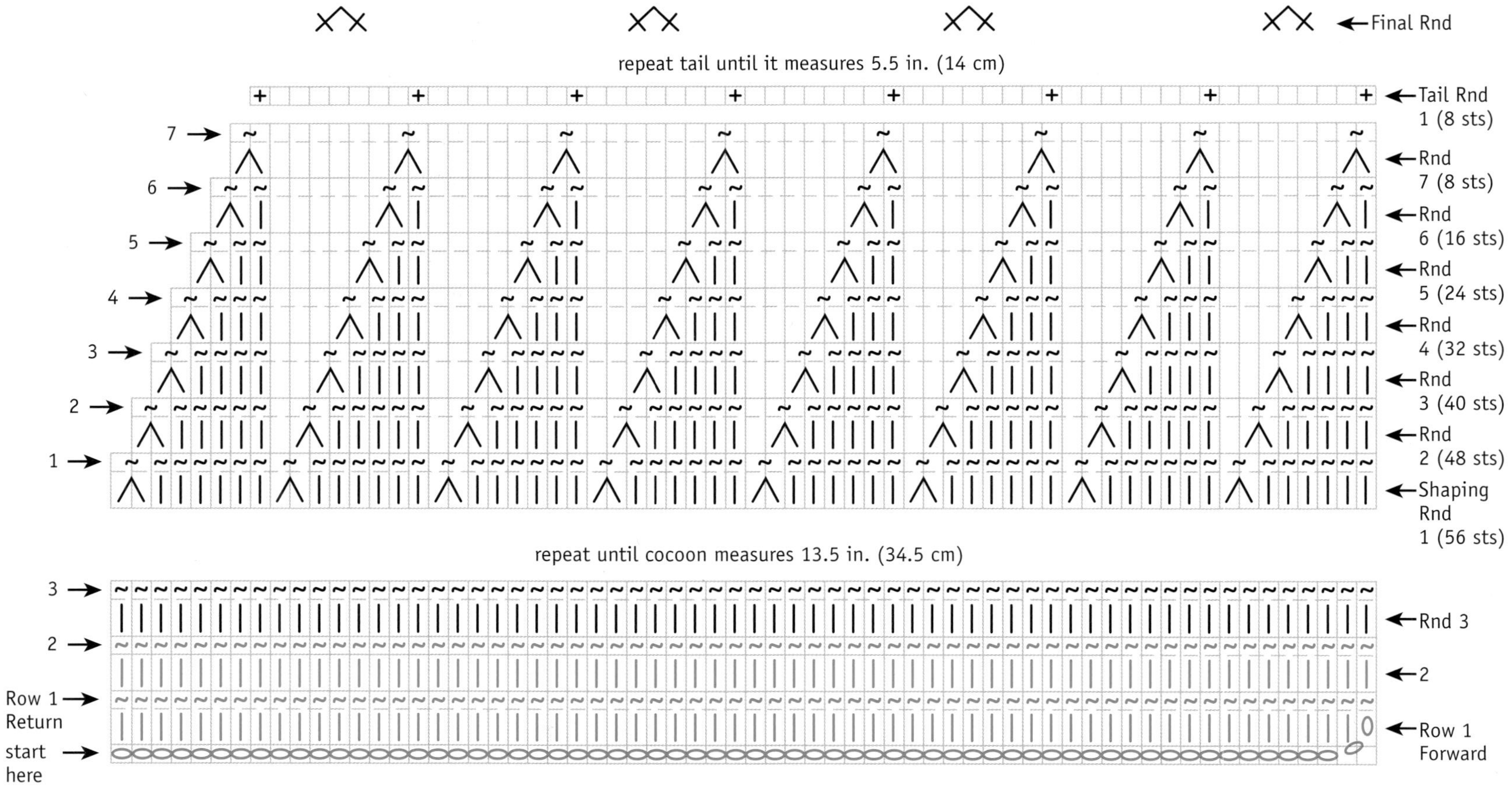

Final Rnd

Tail Rnd 1 (8 sts)
Rnd 7 (8 sts)
Rnd 6 (16 sts)
Rnd 5 (24 sts)
Rnd 4 (32 sts)
Rnd 3 (40 sts)
Rnd 2 (48 sts)
Shaping Rnd 1 (56 sts)

repeat tail until it measures 5.5 in. (14 cm)

repeat until cocoon measures 13.5 in. (34.5 cm)

Rnd 3
2
Row 1 Forward

7
6
5
4
3
2
1

3
2
Row 1 Return
start here

O chain stitch   + single crochet | Tunisian simple stitch

∧ Tunisian simple stitch 2 together   ⌐ return   ✕✕ single crochet 2 together

With second ball of B, yo, pull through 1 lp, *yo, pull through 2 lps. Repeat from * until 3 lps remain on hook. This is the return pass. (You can think of it as "chasing" the forward pass on the inside of the cocoon.)

Rotate project back the other way, slide stitches to other end of hook, and work a Tss in each remaining st of Row 2. When you get to the end of the forward pass, form the finished work into a circle, being careful not to twist it. Tss in first vertical bar from previous row. Place marker.

Starting return pass

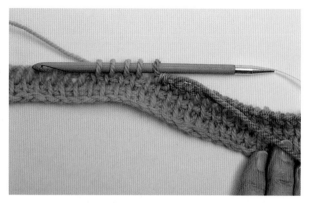

Resume forward pass

Continuing return pass

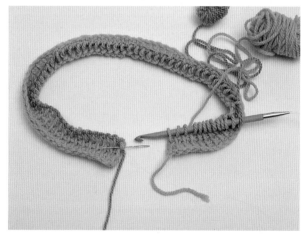

The needle shows where to join to beginning of round

The stitch marker shows the join

NOTE Only the first stitch at the beginning of the *first* return pass is "yo, pull through 1 lp." All subsequent return pass stitches, including the first stitch every time you turn the hook to begin the return pass stitches, are "yo, pull through 2 lps."

Continue to work around the cocoon a bit at a time in spiral fashion, working Tss in each st until you have a comfortable number of sts on your hook, then rotating the piece to work the return pass on the stitches you have made. Always leave at least 3 lps between the return pass and the forward pass so that your return pass does not overtake the forward pass. Move the marker up every time you complete a round. Each round should have 64 sts.

Work in the round until cocoon measures approximately 13.5 in. (34.5 cm) from beginning. Leave several lps for the return pass on the hook; shaping continues in the round.

Shaping

NOTE Continue working in the round as before, keeping the return pass within a few stitches of the forward pass but not overtaking it. You will have to rotate the hook back and forth more frequently as the number of stitches per round decreases. Move the marker to the first stitch of each new round so you can check your stitch count.

Round 1: *Tss in next 6 sts, Tss2tog. Repeat from * around—56 sts.

Round 2: *Tss in next 5 sts, Tss2tog. Repeat from * around—48 sts.

Round 3: *Tss in next 4 sts, Tss2tog. Repeat from * around—40 sts.

Round 4: *Tss in next 3 sts, Tss2tog. Repeat from * around—32 sts.

Round 5: *Tss in next 2 sts, Tss2tog. Repeat from * around—24 sts.

Round 6: *Tss in next st, Tss2tog. Repeat from *
around—16 sts.

Round 7: *Tss2tog. Repeat from * around—8 lps.
On return pass, continue until 1 lp remains. Cut
return pass yarn, leaving a 4-inch tail.

Tail

Round 1: Rotate work to go forward again. Sc in next
8 sts, inserting hook into each st as for Tss—8 sts.

Round 2: Sc in each sc—8 sts.

Repeat Round 2, working in a continuous spiral, until
tail is approximately 5.5 in. (14 cm) long.

Final round: [Sc2tog] 4 times. Fasten off, leaving a
4-inch (10-cm) tail.

Finishing

Turn cocoon inside out. Sew end of tail closed. With
tapestry needle and tail from A, sew ends of first two
rows of cocoon together. Weave in ends. Turn right side
out. Tie a loose knot in the tail of the cocoon where the
tapering begins.

Hat

With A and Tunisian crochet hook (if you want to use
your double-ended hook, just use one end), ch 32.

Row 1 (RS): Tss in second ch from hook and in each ch
across—32 lps on hook. Return.

Row 2: Sk first vertical bar. *Tss in next st. Repeat from
* across—32 lps on hook. Return.

Repeat Row 2 until piece measures 4.5 in. (11.5 cm).

Shaping

Row 1: Sk first vertical bar. Tss in next 2 sts, Tss2tog. *Tss
in next 3 sts, Tss2tog. Repeat from * across until 2 sts
remain. Tss in last 2 sts—26 lps on hook. Return.

Row 2: Sk first vertical bar. Tss in next st, Tss2tog. *Tss in
each of next 2 sts, Tss2tog. Repeat from * across until
2 sts remain. Tss in last 2 sts—20 lps on hook. Return.

Row 3: Sk first vertical bar. Tss2tog. *Tss in next st,
Tss2tog. Repeat from * until 2 sts remain. Tss in last 2
sts—14 lps on hook. Return.

Row 4: Sk first vertical bar. *Tss2tog. Repeat from * until
1 st remains. Tss in final st—8 lps on hook. Return.

Row 5: Sk first vertical bar. Sc in each st across, inserting
hook into each st as for Tss—7 sts. Turn.

Row 6: Ch 1, [sc2tog] 3 times, sc in last st. Turn.

Row 7: Ch 1, [sc2tog] twice. Fasten off, leaving a long
enough tail to sew top and back seam closed.

Finishing

Thread tail into tapestry needle. With WS facing you, sew
top of hat closed, then sew back seam closed. Weave in
remaining ends.

Hat

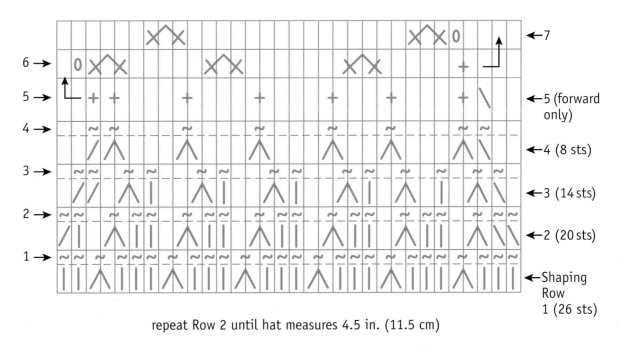

6 →
5 →
4 →
3 →
2 →
1 →

←7
←5 (forward only)
←4 (8 sts)
←3 (14 sts)
←2 (20 sts)
←Shaping Row 1 (26 sts)

repeat Row 2 until hat measures 4.5 in. (11.5 cm)

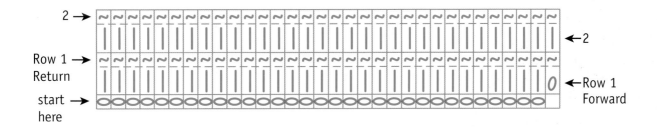

2 →
Row 1 → Return
start → here

←2
←Row 1 Forward

O chain stitch   **+** single crochet   **~** return   ↑ turn

Λ Tunisian simple stitch 2 together   **|** Tunisian simple stitch   **XX** Single crochet 2 together

Christening Gown, Bonnet, and Booties

This sweet heirloom set combines Tunisian crossed stitches with Tunisian knit stitches for texture and visual interest. Picot trim adds just the right finishing touch.

MEASUREMENTS

One size fits 3–6 months. Chest circumference: 18 in. (46 cm); finished length: 29 in. (73.5 cm), including trim

Bonnet circumference 13 in. (33 cm). Bootie foot length 4 in. (10 cm)

MATERIALS

Lion Brand Jamie (100% acrylic; 1.75 oz./50 g; 137 yd./125 m)

Light

Angel white (100), 8 skeins for gown, 1 skein for both bonnet and booties

U.S. size H-8 (5.0 mm) Tunisian crochet hook (or size needed to obtain gauge) for gown skirt and for bonnet and booties

U.S. size J-10 (6.0 mm) Tunisian crochet hook for gown bodice

U.S. size F-5 (3.75 mm) regular crochet hook (or size needed to keep back seam placket and trim flat)

Stitch marker

5 yd. (4.6 m) double-face feather-edge ribbon, ³⁄₈ in. (9 mm) wide

Tapestry needle

GAUGE

19 sts and 17 rows in Tunisian cross stitch pattern (Rows 3–6 of Skirt) with Tunisian size H-8 hook = 4 in. (10 cm)

Special Stitches

Make 1 (M1): Insert hook from front to back in space before next st, yo, pull up lp—1 st increased.

Tunisian cross stitch (X-st): Sk next vertical bar, Tss in next vertical bar. Working in front of st just made, Tss in the skipped vertical bar (the one immediately before the one where you just made the Tss).

NOTE To make it easier to find the skipped vertical bar, gently stretch the work.

Tunisian knit stitch 2 together (Tks2tog): Insert hook through next 2 sts at same time, with hook ending at back of work as for Tks. Yo, pull up lp—1 st decreased.

Tunisian simple stitch 2 together (Tss2tog): Insert hook through next 2 sts at the same time, with hook ending at front of work as for Tss. Yo, pull up lp—1 st decreased.

Notes

1. The skirt of the gown is worked sideways in one piece; the first and last rows will be joined to form the back seam, then the top edge of the piece formed will be gathered for the waist.

2. See pages 126–131 for step-by-step photos and instructions for Make 1, Tunisian cross stitch, and Tunisian knit stitch 2 together.

Christening Gown

Skirt

With size H-8 Tunisian crochet hook, ch 110.

Row 1: Tss in second ch from hook and in each ch across—110 lps on hook. Return.

Row 2: Sk first vertical bar. Tks in each st across to last st; Tss in final st. Return.

Row 3: Sk first vertical bar. *X-st in next 2 vertical bars. Repeat from * to last vertical bar. Tss in last vertical bar—110 lps on hook. Return.

Row 4: Repeat Row 3.

Row 5: Sk first vertical bar. Tks in each st across—110 lps on hook. Return.

Row 6: Repeat Row 5.

The back (WS) will begin to show a series of ridges.

Repeat Rows 3–6 until skirt measures approximately 33 in. (84 cm).

Repeat Rows 3–5 once more.

Final Row: Sk first vertical bar. *Sc in each st across, inserting hook into each st as for Tks—109 sc.

Do not fasten off.

NOTE If the final row looks too loose, switch to a smaller crochet hook for that row.

Skirt

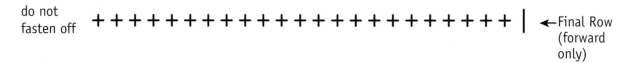

do not
fasten off

←Final Row
(forward
only)

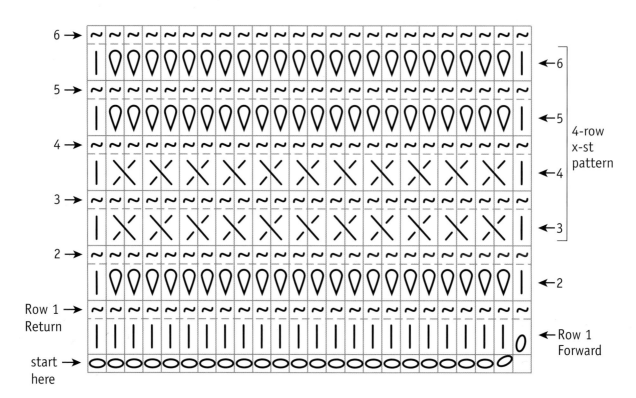

Row 1 →
Return

start →
here

4-row
x-st
pattern

←6

←5

←4

←3

←2

←Row 1
Forward

←Row 1
Forward

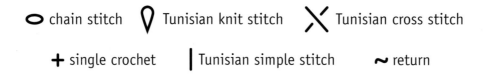

○ chain stitch   ◊ Tunisian knit stitch   ✕ Tunisian cross stitch

✚ single crochet | Tunisian simple stitch   ～ return

SKIRT GATHERS

With Tunisian crochet hook and with RS of work facing you, turn skirt 90 degrees so the row you just finished is now the right-hand side. You will work along the row ends, which are now the top, to create the gathered waist.

Row 1: Work 162 Tss evenly across row ends of skirt—162 lps. Return.

> **NOTE** If necessary, M1 or Tss2tog to get to 162 lps.

Row 2: Sk first vertical bar. *Tss in each st across.

Return: *Yo, pull through 3 lps, yo, pull through 4 lps. Repeat from * until 2 lps remain on hook. Yo, pull through both lps.

> **NOTE** Row 2 Return differs from the standard return.

Row 3: Sk first vertical bar. *Insert hook in top of next group of loops, yo, pull up lp. Repeat from * across until 1 st remains. Tss in final st—65 lps on hook. Return (standard return).

Skirt Gathers

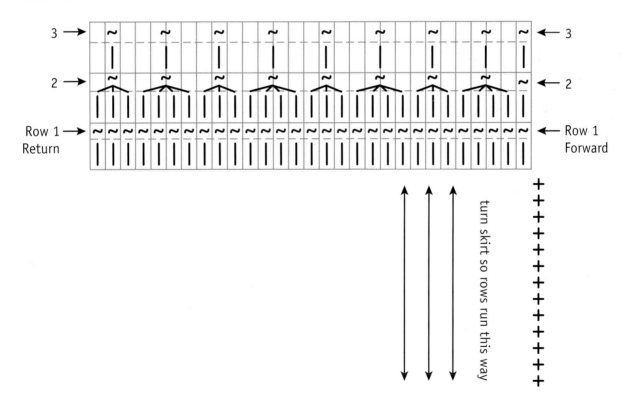

+ single crochet | Tunisian simple stitch   ~ return

⁀ yo, pull through 3 on return   ⁀ yo, pull through 4 on return

Bodice Front

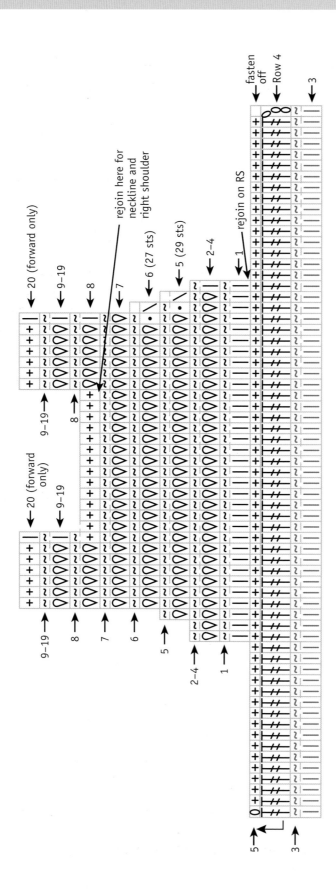

- ○ chain stitch
- ○ Tunisian knit stitch
- • slip stitch
- | Tunisian simple stitch
- + single crochet
- ‡ treble crochet
- ∿ return
- ⌐ turn

20 (forward only)
9–19
8
7
rejoin here for neckline and right shoulder
6 (27 sts)
5 (29 sts)
2–4
1
rejoin on RS
fasten off
Row 4
3

Row 4: Ch 3 (counts as tr). Sk sp between first and second vertical bars; tr in sp between second and third vertical bars. *Tr in next sp between vertical bars. Repeat from * across, tr in final st—65 tr.

Row 5: Ch 1, turn. Sc in each st across—65 sc. Fasten off. Place marker in final st.

Bodice

FRONT

Row 1: With RS of skirt facing you, and size J-10 Tunisian hook, sk first 16 sc of previous row. Join yarn in next st (counts as 1 lp). *Tss in next 32 sts—33 lps on hook. Return.

Row 2: Sk first vertical bar. *Tks in next st. Repeat from * to end—33 lps on hook. Return.

Rows 3–4: Repeat Row 2.

Row 5 (begin armhole shaping): Sk first vertical bar. Sl st in each of next 2 sts, inserting hook into each st as for Tks. Tks across to last 2 sts; leave last 2 sts unworked—29 lps on hook. Return.

Row 6: Sk first vertical bar. Sl st in next st, inserting hook into st as for Tks. Tks in each st across to last st; leave last st unworked—27 lps on hook. Return.

Row 7: Sk first vertical bar. Tks in each st across—27 lps on hook. Return.

Row 8 (start left shoulder): Sk first vertical bar. Tks in next 6 sts. Leave remaining sts unworked—7 lps on hook. Return.

Row 9: Sk first vertical bar. Tks in next 6 sts—7 lps on hook. Return.

Rows 10–19: Repeat Row 9.

Row 20: Sk first vertical bar. Sc in each st across, inserting hook into each stitch as for Tks—6 sc. Fasten off.

NECKLINE AND RIGHT SHOULDER

Row 8: Join yarn in last st worked on Row 8 of left shoulder. *Sc in next st, inserting hook into st as for Tks. Repeat from * across until 6 sts remain. Tks in remaining sts—7 lps on hook. Return.

Row 9: Sk first vertical bar. Tks in next 6 sts—7 lps on hook. Return.

Rows 10–19: Repeat Row 9.

Row 20: Sk first vertical bar. Sc in each st across, inserting hook into each stitch as for Tks—6 sc. Fasten off.

LEFT BACK BODICE

Row 1: With RS facing, and size J-10 Tunisian hook, join yarn in marked st from end of Row 5 of skirt gathers (first unworked st—a sc). *Insert hook in next st, pull up lp. Repeat from * in each unworked sc—16 lps on hook. Return.

Row 2: Sk first vertical bar. *Tks in next st. Repeat from * across—16 lps on hook. Return.

Rows 3–4: Repeat Row 2.

Row 5 (begin armhole shaping): Sk first vertical bar. Tks in each st across to last 2 sts; leave last 2 sts unworked—14 lps on hook. Return.

Row 6: Sk first vertical bar. Tks in each st across to last st; leave final st unworked—13 lps on hook. Return.

Row 7: Sk first vertical bar. Tks in each st across—13 lps on hook. Return.

Rows 8–17: Repeat Row 7.

Row 18: Sk first vertical bar. Sl st in next 6 sts, inserting hook into each st as for Tks. Tks in each remaining st—7 lps on hook. Return.

Row 19: Sk first vertical bar. Tks in each st across—7 lps on hook. Return.

Row 20: Sk first vertical bar. Sc in each st across, inserting hook into each stitch as for Tks—6 sc. Fasten off.

RIGHT BACK BODICE

Row 1: With RS facing, and size J-10 Tunisian hook, join yarn in first unworked st on Row 1 of Front Bodice (after the bodice stitches that are worked into Row 5 of skirt gathers). Tks in next 15 sts (to end of row)—16 lps on hook. Return.

Row 2: Sk first vertical bar. *Tks in next st. Repeat from * across—16 lps on hook. Return.

Rows 3–4: Repeat Row 2.

Row 5 (begin armhole shaping): Sk first vertical bar. Sl st in next 2 sts, inserting hook into each st as for Tks. Tks in each st across—14 lps on hook. Return.

Row 6: Sk first vertical bar. Sl st in next st, inserting hook into st as for Tks. Tks in each st across—13 lps on hook. Return.

Row 7: Sk first vertical bar. Tks in each st across—13 lps on hook. Return.

Rows 8–17: Repeat Row 7.

Left Back Bodice

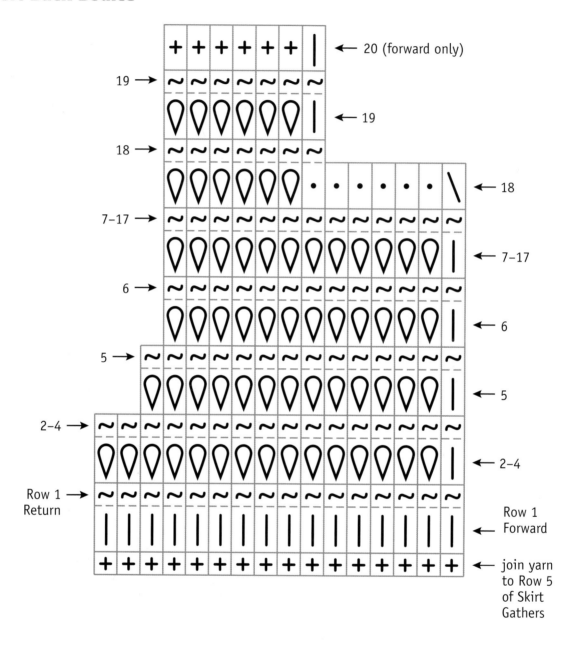

20 (forward only)

19

18

7–17

6

5

2–4

Row 1 Return

Row 1 Forward

join yarn to Row 5 of Skirt Gathers

| Tunisian simple stitch   ᓄ Tunisian knit stitch   + single crochet

• slip stitch   ~ return

Right Back Bodice

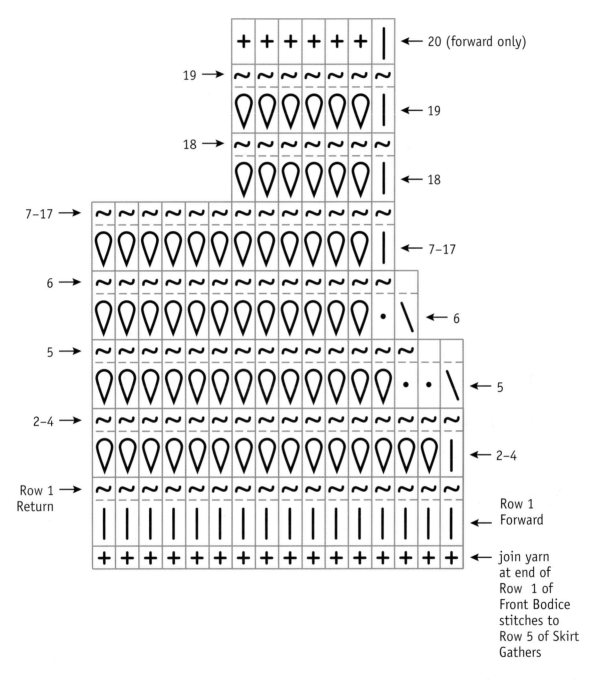

← 20 (forward only)

19 →

← 19

18 →

← 18

7–17 →

← 7–17

6 →

← 6

5 →

← 5

2–4 →

← 2–4

Row 1 Return →

Row 1 Forward →

← join yarn at end of Row 1 of Front Bodice stitches to Row 5 of Skirt Gathers

| Tunisian simple stitch   ♀ Tunisian knit stitch   + single crochet

• slip stitch   ∼ return

Row 18: Sk first vertical bar. Tks in next 6 sts, leaving remaining sts unworked—7 lps on hook. Return.

Row 19: Sk first vertical bar. Tks in each st across—7 lps on hook. Leave remaining sts unworked. Return.

Row 20: Sk first vertical bar. Sc in each st across, inserting hook into each stitch as for Tks—6 sc. Fasten off.

Assembly

Gently steam block on WS. With tapestry needle, weave in ends.

With WS facing, sew underarm seams.

BACK EDGING AND HEM

With RS facing and using size F-5 crochet hook (or size needed to keep placket flat), join yarn in top corner of back left bodice (inner corner, which goes down center of back). Ch 1. Sc evenly down edge of bodice and skirt, working 3 sc around end of tr row at waist. Work 3 sc in bottom corner, then continue in sc across bottom of skirt and up other side of back (again working 3 sc in corner and around end of tr row at waist). Fasten off.

> **NOTE** You may need to switch to a larger crochet hook across bottom of skirt if necessary to keep hem flat.

Lightly steam block back and hem on WS.

With WS facing you, line up back seam edges. Pin in place if necessary to keep the two sides aligned. Starting at bottom, sew seam, stopping after approximately 18 in. (46 cm) to leave the entire back of the bodice and approximately 4 in. (10 cm) below the waist unseamed. Fasten off.

With WS facing, sew shoulder seams.

Sleeves

Foundation row: With RS facing, using size F-5 crochet hook, join yarn at underarm seam. Ch 1 (counts as sc). Work 42 sc evenly around sleeve opening—43 sts. Join to first sc with sl st.

> **NOTE** You will need a multiple of 7 sts + 1 for the sleeve trim to come out even.

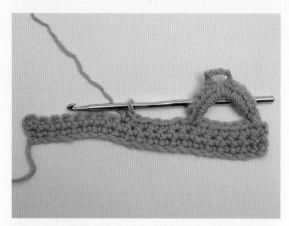

The Sleeve Trim, Step by Step

Start of second arch

Trim Row 1 moving from right to left

Trim Row 1 turned to go back the other way

Trim Row 1 turned again to continue forward

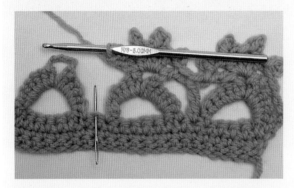

Trim Row 2 (needle indicates placement for treble crochet)

Row 1 (WS): Ch 1, turn. Sc in next 6 sts. *Turn, ch 7, sk 5 sc, sc in next sc, turn. Work [6 sc, ch 5, 6 sc] in ch-7 sp, **sc in next 7 sc of Foundation Row. Repeat from * around, ending last repeat at **; sc in next st. Leave final st unworked.

Row 2 (RS): Ch 4, turn. *Sk to next ch-5 lp, [dc, ch 3, sl st in first ch of ch-3 just made] 4 times in ch-5 lp, dc in same ch-5 lp. Tr in next unworked sc between arches on Row 1. Repeat from * around. Do not join last arch to first arch. Fasten off.

Repeat with other sleeve.

Skirt Trim

> **NOTE** You will need a multiple of 7 sts for the trim to come out even. Sample gown has 161 sc. If your count is off, sc one stitch more or less in Row 1 where instructions say "sc in next 7 foundation sc," and skip one sc more or less where you would normally skip 5 to correspond. Make sure there is still 1 unworked sc in between the end of each arch and the beginning of the next. If you need more than one adjustment, space them evenly around the hem to arrive at the correct multiple.

Row 1: With F-5 hook and WS facing, join yarn in bottom edge at back seam. Ch 1, sc in next 6 sts. *Turn, ch 7, sk 5 sc, sc in next sc, turn. Work [6 sc, ch 5, 6 sc] in ch-7 sp, **sc in next 7 foundation sc. Repeat from * around, ending last repeat at **; sc in next st. You should have 1 unworked sc between the end of that arch and the beginning of the first arch.

Hem and Sleeve Trim

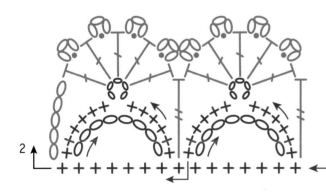

2

Row 1 (turns internally)

○ chain stitch   ✛ single crochet   ┬ double crochet

• slip stitch   treble crochet   ↱ turn

Row 2 (RS): Turn. Ch 4. *Sk to next ch-5 lp, [dc, ch 3, sl st in first ch of ch-3 just made] 4 times in ch-5 lp, dc in same ch-5 lp. Tr in next unworked sc between arches on Row 1. Repeat from * around. Do not join last arch to first arch. Fasten off.

Neckline Trim

Row 1: With WS facing and size F-5 crochet hook, join yarn at top back corner of head opening. Sc evenly around neckline to other corner.

Row 2: Ch 1, turn. Sc in first 3 sc, *(ch 3, sl st in first ch), sc in next 3 sc. Repeat from *. Fasten off.

Back Ties

There are three sets of ties (six ties total): one at the back neck, one above the back waist openwork, and one below the back waist openwork. Make each tie the same way.

Join yarn where tie should go. Sc in same stitch as joining, working around yarn end to help hold it in place. Ch 45. Sc in second ch from hook and in each ch. Sl st in beg sc. Fasten off.

Repeat for other five ties. With tapestry needle, weave in ends, making sure tie is secure. Lightly steam block ties if desired.

Neckline Trim

2 ↑ 0 ++++++++
  └ 0 +++++++++ ←Row 1

○ chain stitch   + single crochet   • slip stitch   ↑ turn

Ties

← Row 1

0 chain stitch + single crochet

join to garment

Ribbon Embellishment

Cut approximately 64 in. (163 cm) of ribbon. Starting at center front above gathers, weave ribbon in and out through treble crochets of Row 4. Leave ends loose until gown is on baby and back ties are tied, then tie ribbon in front.

Bonnet

NOTE The bonnet starts at the back with rounds of regular crochet. The Tunisian crochet pattern begins after Round 4.

With size H-8 Tunisian crochet hook, ch 3.

Round 1 (RS): Work 11 hdc in third ch from hook (other 2 chs count as first hdc). Join to top of beg ch-2 with sl st—12 sts.

Round 2: Ch 2 (counts as hdc). Hdc in st at base of chs, *2 hdc in next st. Repeat from * around. Join to top of beg ch-2 with sl st—24 sts.

Round 3: Ch 2 (counts as hdc). 2 hdc in next st. *Hdc in next st, 2 hdc in next st. Repeat from * around. Join to top of beg ch-2 with sl st—36 sts.

Round 4: Ch 2 (counds as hdc). Hdc in next st, 2 hdc in next st. *Hdc in next 2 sts, 2 hdc in next st. Repeat from * around. Join to top of beg ch-2 with sl st— 48 sts.

Row 5 (Tunisian crochet): Tss in next st and in next 34 sts—36 lps on hook. Return.

NOTE For Row 5 you will be inserting the hook under the top 2 threads of the sc stitches since there are no vertical bars in sc.

Row 6: Sk first vertical bar. *X-st in next 2 vertical bars. Repeat from * to last vertical bar. Tss in last vertical bar—36 lps on hook. Return.

NOTE The bonnet will look bunched up as you work the first few Tunisian rows. It will straighten out on subsequent rows.

Row 7: Repeat Row 6.

Row 8: Sk first vertical bar. Tks in each st across—36 lps on hook. Return.

Row 9: Repeat Row 8.

Rows 10–17: Repeat Rows 6–9 twice.

Round 18: Ch 1. Sk first vertical bar. Sc in each st across, inserting hook into each st as for Tks—35 sc. Ch 3 (counts as tr) and continue along neckline of bonnet in tr—29 tr. Join to beg ch with sl st.

Row 19 (WS): Ch 1, turn. Sc in each tr across bonnet neckline—28 sc. Work 3 sc around post of final tr. Continue around the face of the bonnet. Sc in next st. *Ch 3, sl st in first ch (picot made), sc in next 3 sts. Repeat from * across. Join to beg ch with sl st. Fasten off.

Finishing

With tapestry needle, weave in ends. Lightly steam block on WS.

Cut approximately 48 in. (122 cm) of ribbon. Weave in and out of tr from front neckline, around back of neck, to other front neckline. Let ribbon ends dangle or tie them as desired.

Bonnet Back

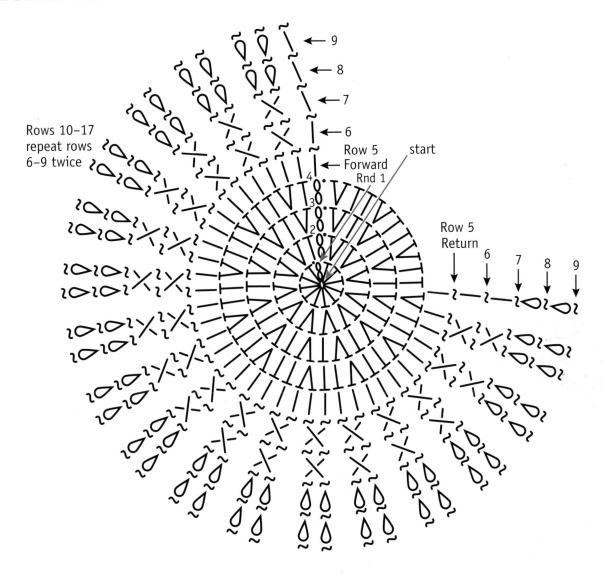

Rows 10–17
repeat rows
6–9 twice

← 9
← 8
← 7
← 6
Row 5
← Forward
Rnd 1

start

Row 5
Return

6   7   8   9

O chain stitch   T half double crochet   Ø Tunisian knit stitch

X Tunisian cross stitch | Tunisian simple stitch   ~ return

Bonnet Finishing

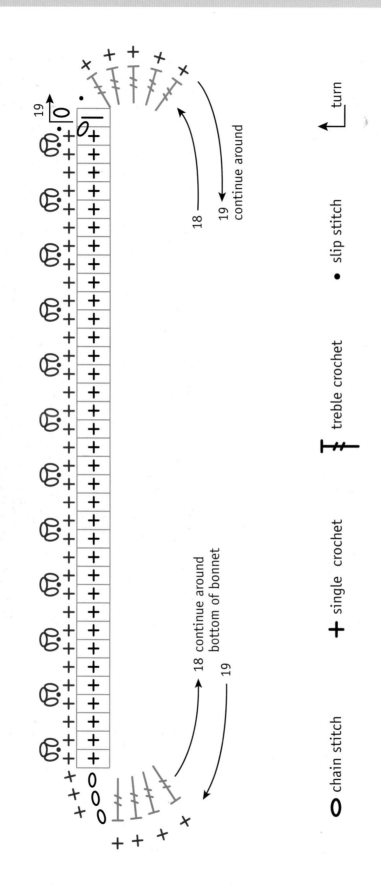

19

18

19
continue around

18 continue around
bottom of bonnet

19

turn

• slip stitch

treble crochet

+ single crochet

0 chain stitch

Booties

NOTE Each bootie is made in two pieces: the sole and the upper. The upper part is then seamed at the back heel and attached to the sole.

Sole (make 2)

NOTE Sole starts at the heel and is shaped toward the toe.

With size H-8 Tunisian crochet hook, ch 5.

Row 1 (RS): Tks in second ch from hook and in each ch across—5 lps on hook. Return.

Row 2: Sk first vertical bar. Tks in each st across—5 lps on hook. Return.

Row 3: Sk first vertical bar. M1, Tks in next 3 sts, M1, Tks in final st—7 lps on hook. Return.

Row 4: Sk first vertical bar. Tks in each st across—7 lps on hook. Return.

Row 5: Sk first vertical bar. M1, Tks in next 5 sts, M1, Tks in final st—9 lps on hook. Return.

Rows 6–11: Sk first vertical bar. Tks in each st across—9 lps on hook. Return.

Row 12: Sk first vertical bar. M1, Tks in next 7 sts, M1, Tks in final st—11 lps on hook. Return.

Rows 13–15: Sk first vertical bar. Tks in each st across—11 lps on hook. Return.

Row 16: Sk first vertical bar. Tks2tog, Tks in next 5 sts, Tks2tog, Tks in final st—9 lps on hook. Return.

Row 17: Sk first vertical bar. Tks in each st across—9 lps on hook. Return.

Row 18: Sk first vertical bar. Tks2tog, Tks in next 3 sts, Tks2tog, Tks in final st—7 lps on hook. Return.

Round 19: Sk first vertical bar. Sc in each st across, inserting hook into each st as for Tks. At end of row, continue around sole, working sc in ends of rows and in unworked loops of foundation chain. Join to first sc with sl st. Fasten off.

Upper (make 2)

NOTE The X-st pattern in this piece is different from the one used in the gown and bonnet (X-sts on each row instead of two rows of X-st followed by 2 rows of Tks).

Ch 50.

Row 1 (RS): Tks in second ch from hook and in each ch across—50 lps on hook. Return.

Bootie Sole

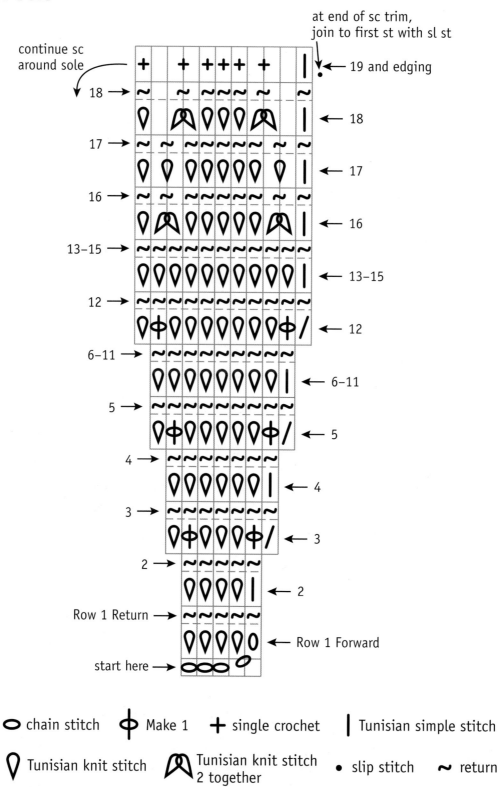

continue sc around sole

at end of sc trim, join to first st with sl st

← 19 and edging

18

17

16

13–15

12

6–11

5

4

3

2

Row 1 Return → Row 1 Forward

start here →

○ chain stitch   ⬥ Make 1   ✛ single crochet | Tunisian simple stitch

◗ Tunisian knit stitch   ⋏ Tunisian knit stitch 2 together   • slip stitch   ～ return

Bootie Upper

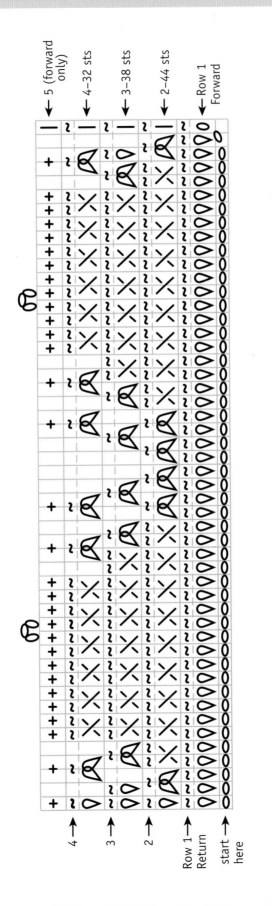

5 (forward only)

4–32 sts

3–38 sts

2–44 sts

Row 1 Forward

4

3

2

Row 1 Return

start here

0 chain stitch $+$ single crochet $|$ Tunisian simple stitch $\times$ Tunisian cross stitch

0 Tunisian knit stitch $\mathcal{A}$ Tunisian knit stitch 2 together $\mathcal{c}$ return

Row 2: Sk first vertical bar. Tks2tog, [X-st in next 2 vertical bars] 9 times, Tks2tog 4 times, [X-st in next 2 vertical bars] 9 times, Tks2tog, Tks in final st—44 lps on hook. Return.

Row 3: Sk first vertical bar. Tks in next st, Tks2tog, [X-st in next 2 vertical bars] 7 times, Tks2tog 4 times, [X-st in next 2 vertical bars] 7 times, Tks2tog, Tks in last 2 sts—38 lps on hook. Return.

Row 4: Sk first vertical bar. Tks2tog, [X-st in next 2 vertical bars] 6 times, Tks2tog 4 times, [X-st in next 2 vertical bars] 6 times, Tks2tog, Tks in final st—32 lps on hook.

Row 5: Sk first vertical bar. Sc in next 9 sts, inserting hook into each st as for Tks, ch 3, sc in next 12 sts, inserting hook into each st as for Tks, ch 3, sc in remaining 10 sts, inserting hook into each st as for Tks—32 sc, 2 ch-3 sps.
Fasten off.

Finishing

With tapestry needle, weave in ends. With WS facing, sew back heel seam.

Turn top of bootie right side out. Position it on sole, making sure that RS of sole faces outward and heel of bootie top is at wide part of sole. Seam all around.

Cut 24 in. (61 cm) of ribbon for each bootie. Thread through ch-3 lps of Row 5. Tie in a bow.

Strappy Pants

These comfortable, easy-care pants with suspenders are worked from the waist down, one leg at a time. The straps are sewn in the back and attach with Velcro in the front. Cross the straps in the back to shorten them, then have your child wear them straight over each shoulder as he or she grows.

MEASUREMENTS

Pattern is for sizes 6, 9, and 12 months. Instructions are for smallest size, with larger sizes in parentheses

MATERIALS

Plymouth Maria Diaz Maciel (90% fine superwash wool, 10% baby alpaca; 7 oz./200 g; 437 yd./400 m)

Medium

Waters (0103), 1 skein

U.S. size K-10½ (6.5 mm) Tunisian hook (or size needed to obtain gauge)

U.S. size H-8 (5.0 mm) crochet hook

Tapestry needle

Velcro fastener, 0.75 by 8 in. (2 by 20 cm), as close to yarn color as is available

Sewing thread to match color of yarn

Sewing needle

GAUGE

14 sts and 10 rows in Tss = 4 in. (10 cm), blocked

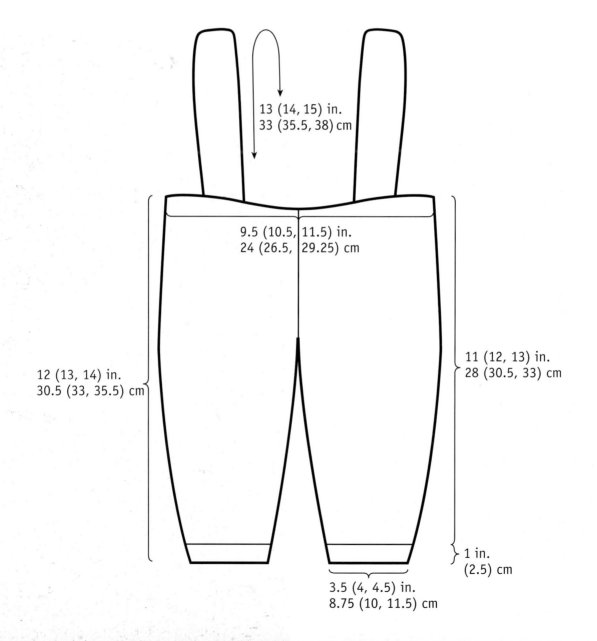

13 (14, 15) in.
33 (35.5, 38) cm

9.5 (10.5, 11.5) in.
24 (26.5, 29.25) cm

11 (12, 13) in.
28 (30.5, 33) cm

12 (13, 14) in.
30.5 (33, 35.5) cm

1 in.
(2.5) cm

3.5 (4, 4.5) in.
8.75 (10, 11.5) cm

Special Stitch

Tunisian simple stitch 2 together (Tss2tog): Insert hook through next 2 sts at same time, with hook remaining at front of work as for Tss. Yo, pull up lp—1 st decreased.

Note

The pants are worked one leg at a time from the waist down.

Pattern

Pant Leg (make 2)

Ch 38 (42, 46).

Row 1: Tps in second ch from hook and in each ch across—38 (42, 46) lps on hook. Return.

Row 2: Sk first vertical bar. Tps in each st across to final st, Tss in final st—38 (42, 46) lps on hook. Return.

Row 3: Repeat Row 2.

Rows 4–21 (4–23, 4–25): Sk first vertical bar. Tss in each st across. Return.

Row 22 (24, 26): Sk first vertical bar. Tss2tog, Tss in each st across to last 3 sts, Tss2tog, Tss in final st—36 (40, 44) lps on hook. Return.

Rows 23–24 (25–26, 27–28): Sk first vertical bar. Tss in each st across. Return.

Row 25 (27, 29): Repeat Row 22—34 (38, 42) lps on hook.

Rows 26–27 (28–29, 30–31): Repeat Rows 23–24.

Row 28 (30, 32): Repeat Row 22—32 (36, 40) lps on hook.

Rows 29–30 (31–32, 33–34): Repeat Rows 23–24.

Row 31 (33, 35): Repeat Row 22—30 (34, 38) lps on hook.

Rows 32–33 (34–35, 36–37): Repeat Rows 23–24.

Row 34 (36, 38): Repeat Row 22—28 (32, 36) lps on hook.

Rows 35–36 (37–40, 39–44): Repeat Rows 23–24.

Rows 37–38 (41–42, 45–46): Sk first vertical bar. Tps in each st across to final st, Tss in final st. Return.

Row 39 (43, 47): Sk first vertical bar. Sc in each st across, inserting hook into each st as for Tps—27 (31, 35) sc. Fasten off.

Strap (make 2)

With regular crochet hook, ch 6.

Row 1: Sc in second ch from hook and in each ch across—5 sts.

Rows 2–53 (2–57, 2–61): Ch 1, turn. Sc in each sc across.

Edging Row: Ch 1. Working in ends of rows and in unworked loops of foundation chain, sc down long side of piece, across bottom edge, and up other long side. Sc in each st across top edge. Sl st in beg ch to join. Fasten off.

Pants (Section)

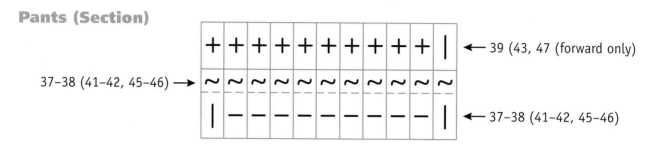

37–38 (41–42, 45–46) →

← 39 (43, 47 (forward only)

← 37–38 (41–42, 45–46)

repeat 1 decrease row,
2 rows even, through Row 36 (40, 44)

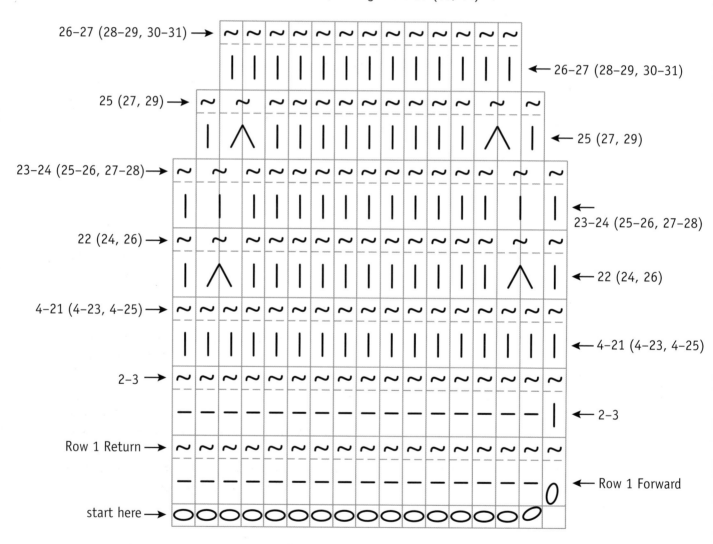

26–27 (28–29, 30–31) →

← 26–27 (28–29, 30–31)

25 (27, 29) →

← 25 (27, 29)

23–24 (25–26, 27–28) →

← 23–24 (25–26, 27–28)

22 (24, 26) →

← 22 (24, 26)

4–21 (4–23, 4–25) →

← 4–21 (4–23, 4–25)

2–3 →

← 2–3

Row 1 Return →

← Row 1 Forward

start here →

○ chain stitch   — Tunisian purl stitch | Tunisian simple stitch

⋀ Tunisian simple stitch 2 together   + single crochet   ∼ return

Strap

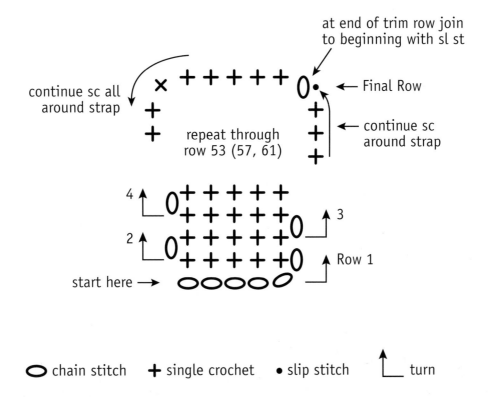

at end of trim row join
to beginning with sl st

continue sc all
around strap

← Final Row

repeat through
row 53 (57, 61)

← continue sc
around strap

4

3

2

Row 1

start here →

○ chain stitch   **+** single crochet   • slip stitch   turn

Finishing

Gently steam block pieces on WS. With tapestry needle,
weave in ends.

Sew inseams: With WS facing, fold one leg in half.
Starting at bottom end of leg opening (narrow end),
sew long edges of piece together for 6 (7, 8) in. (15.25
[17.75, 20.5] cm). Repeat with other leg.

With WS facing, lay both legs next to each other with
inseams toward middle. Sew the two legs together along
front and back seams from crotch to waist.

Turn pants right side out. Position ends of straps on
the inside of the back so they are each halfway between
outer edge and center of back, approximately 1/2 in.
(1.25 cm) below waistband. Pin in place. Using sewing
thread and needle, sew straps in place.

Fold straps into position so you can see where they
should attach in the front. Cut two pieces of hook-and-
loop fabric approximately 1 in. (2.5 cm) wide. Sew the
hook sides on the ends of the straps, just inside the sc
edging. Pin the loop sides to the corresponding position
of the inside front of pants. Sew in place.

Sunny Bow Headband

SKILL LEVEL

EASY

The unusual and attractive stitch pattern used in this headband takes a yarn over and carries it across three subsequent stitches. The interesting fabric it produces is just the right style for a simple headband, topped with a festive bow.

MEASUREMENTS

Width: 2¼ in. (5.75 cm); circumference is adjustable

For premies/newborns, head circumference is approximately 12 in. (30.5 cm); for babies, 14 in. (35.5 cm); and for toddlers, 16 in. (40.5 cm)

MATERIALS

Muench Yarns Family (75% acrylic microfiber, 25% nylon; 1.75 oz./50 g, 83 yd./76 m)

Medium

Yellow (5725), 1 skein

U.S. size J-10 (6.0 mm) Tunisian crochet hook

Tapestry needle

GAUGE

Since the project is so small and you can alter the size by adding rows, there is no need to make a gauge swatch.

Pulling Yarn Over Stitches

Use the fingers of your non-hook hand to pull the yo over the 3 Tss. It will create a horizontal line across the bottom of those stitches.

Band

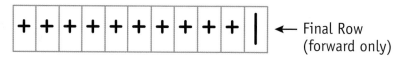

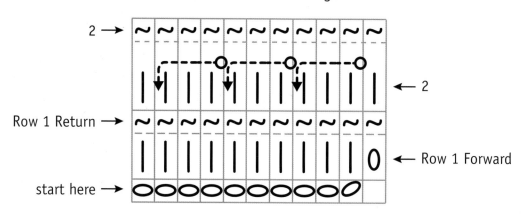

repeat row 2 until
headband is desired length

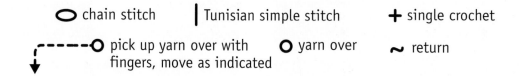

○ chain stitch | Tunisian simple stitch   + single crochet

- - - ○ pick up yarn over with   ○ yarn over   ~ return
fingers, move as indicated

Pattern

Ch 11.

Row 1 (RS): Tss in second ch from hook and in each ch
across—11 lps on hook. Return.

Row 2: Sk first vertical bar. *Yo, Tss in next 3 vertical bars,
pull yo over last 3 lps and off hook. Repeat from *
across until 1 st remains. Tss in final st. Return.

Repeat Row 2 until headband is desired length.

Final Row: Sk first vertical bar. Sc in each st across,
inserting hook into each st as for Tss—10 sc.
Fasten off.

Bow

Ch 15.

Row 1: Tss in second ch from hook and in each ch
across—15 lps on hook. Return.

Row 2: Sk first vertical bar. Tss in each st across. Return.

Rows 3–5: Repeat Row 2.

Row 6: Sk first vertical bar. Sc in each st across, inserting
hook into each st as for Tss—14 sc. Fasten off.

Bow

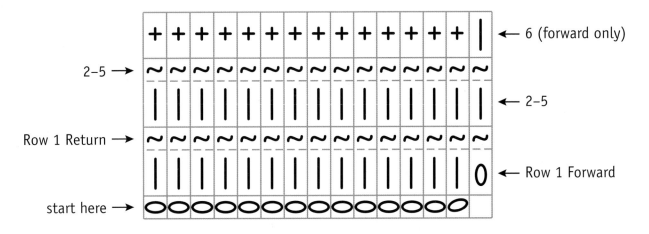

6 (forward only)

2–5 →   ← 2–5

Row 1 Return →   ← Row 1 Forward

start here →

○ chain stitch | Tunisian simple stitch   + single crochet   ~ return

Finishing

Lightly steam block both pieces on WS. Weave in ends.

Thread a tapestry needle with approximately 24 in. (61 cm) of yarn. Take several stitches through the middle of the bow, then pull the yarn tight to gather the bow in the center. Wrap the remaining yarn around the center five or six times, ending with the yarn at the back of the bow. Position bow on RS of headband, slightly off center. Sew in place. Weave in ends.

With WS facing, sew ends of headband together. Weave in ends.

Nursery Box

Cotton yarn in dense Tunisian simple stitch creates sturdy, washable containers ideal for use in a nursery. Vary the main color and trim to fit your decor.

MEASUREMENTS

9½ in. (2 cm) wide by 4½ in. (11.5 cm) long by 3 in. (7.5 cm) high

MATERIALS

Lily Sugar 'n Cream (100% cotton; 2.5 oz./70.9 g, 120 yd./109 m)

Medium

Color A: Hot Pink (01740), 2 balls

Color B: Pinky Stripes (21732), 1 ball

U.S. size G-6 (4.0 mm) Tunisian crochet hook (or size needed to obtain gauge)

U.S. size G-6 (4.0 mm) regular crochet hook (or same size as Tunisian hook)

U.S. size E-4 (3.5 mm) regular crochet hook (or size needed to keep trim flat)

Tapestry needle

GAUGE

Gauge is flexible for this project. Suggested gauge: 18 sts and 14 rows in Tss = 4 in. (10.2 cm), blocked

Special Stitch

Crochet cast-on (CCO): *First CCO:* Bring yarn behind hook. Insert a regular crochet hook from left to right in final st and under the Tunisian hook, yo, pull lp through. Move regular crochet hook to top of Tunisian hook, yo, pull lp through. *Subsequent CCOs:* Move yarn toward you then under and behind hook. Bring regular crochet hook in front of and on top of Tunisian hook. Yo, pull lp through. *Final CCO:* Slip last lp from regular crochet hook back onto Tunisian hook. Rotate Tunisian hook back into normal position and commence return pass.

Note

See page 123 for step-by-step photos and instructions for working crochet cast-on.

Pattern

With A and Tunisian crochet hook, ch 40.

Row 1 (RS): Tss in second ch from hook and in each ch across—40 lps on hook. Return.

Row 2: Sk first vertical bar. *Tss in next st. Repeat from * across—40 lps on hook. Return.

Rows 3–9: Repeat Row 2.

Row 10 (increase row): Ch 11. Tss in second ch from hook and in each of the new chs, then Tss in every st across to end. After final Tss, CCO 11 sts—62 lps on hook. Return.

Rows 11–25: Sk first vertical bar. *Tss in next st. Repeat from * across—62 lps on hook. Return.

Row 26 (decrease row): Sk first vertical bar. Sl st in next 11 sts, inserting hook into each st as for Tss. *Tss in next st. Repeat from * to last 11 sts; leave last 11 sts unworked—40 lps on hook. Return.

Rows 27–34: Repeat Row 2.

Row 35: Sk first vertical bar. Sl st in each st across, inserting hook into each st as for Tss—39 sc. Fasten off.

Rejoin yarn in corner of Row 26 where main part of box meets left-hand side panel. Sl st across 11 unworked sts of Row 26, inserting hook into each st as for Tss—11 sts. Fasten off.

Assembly

Weave in ends. Steam block on WS.

Thread tapestry needle with B. Fold up sides of box. With WS together and RS facing you, whipstitch each corner edge, leaving a long tail at beginning and end. These seams are supposed to be visible; if you prefer them not to show, use A for the whipstitching. With tapestry needle, weave in ends on inside of box after seaming.

Trim

With B and regular crochet hook, and RS facing, join yarn in any corner.

Row 1: Ch 1. Sc in each st around top edge of box. Join to beg ch with sl st.

Row 2: Ch 1, turn. Sc in each st around. Join to beg ch with sl st. Fasten off.

Finishing

With tapestry needle, weave in any remaining ends. Lightly steam block into shape if necessary.

Nursery Box

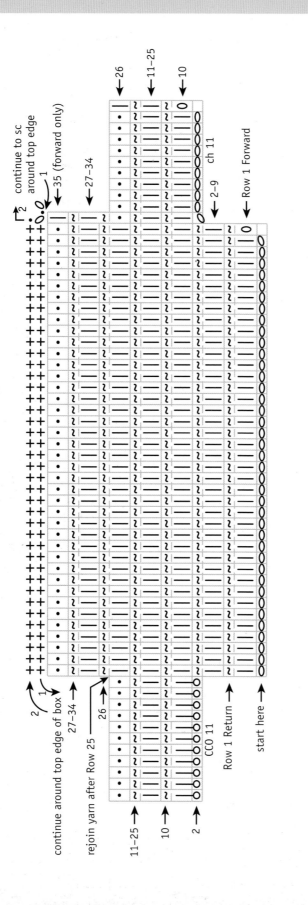

chain stitch

Tunisian simple stitch

slip stitch

return

single crochet

turn

crochet cast-on

Washcloth Quartet

SKILL LEVEL
Simple Stitch
Washcloth and
Knit Washcloth

EASY

SKILL LEVEL
Little Arches
Washcloth and
Checked Washcloth

INTERMEDIATE

Families with babies can never have too many wash-cloths! These colorful, all-cotton washcloths are easy to whip up quickly for yourself or as a gift. The first two use variegated yarn in two different stitch patterns, Tunisian simple stitch and Tunisian knit stitch, for two different looks. The other two cloths use two-color techniques. Make a bunch to keep handy in the Nursery Box.

MEASUREMENTS

7 in. (18 cm) square

MATERIALS

Simple Stitch Washcloth and Knit Washcloth:

Lily Sugar 'n Cream (100% cotton; 2.5 oz./70.9 g, 120 yd./109 m)

Medium

Playtime Ombre (02741), 1 skein for each washcloth

Little Arches Washcloth and Checked Washcloth:

Lily Sugar 'n Cream (100% cotton; 2.5 oz./70.9 g, 120 yd./109 m)

Medium

Color A: White (00001), 1 skein (enough for both washcloths)

Color B: Hot Blue (01742), 1 skein (enough for both washcloths)

All Washcloths

U.S. size J-10 (6.0 mm) Tunisian crochet hook (or size needed to obtain gauge)

Tapestry needle

GAUGE

Gauge is flexible for this project.

Special Stitch

Slip (Sl): Insert hook behind vertical bar of stitch as for Tss, but do not yo and draw up a lp.

NOTE This is not the same as a slip stitch; it just slides the hook through a stitch.

Simple Stitch Washcloth

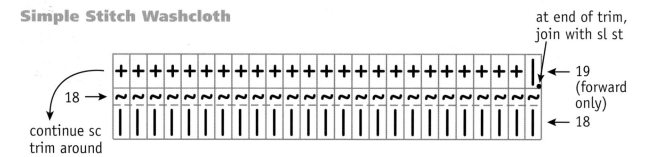

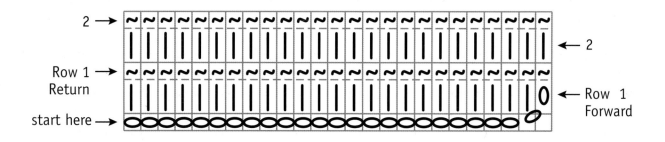

repeat Row 2

 chain stitch   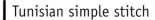 single crochet   • slip stitch | Tunisian simple stitch   ~ return

Simple Stitch Washcloth

Ch 25.

Row 1: Tss in second ch from hook and in each ch across—25 lps on hook. Return.

Row 2: Sk first vertical bar. *Tss in next vertical bar. Repeat from * across. Return.

Rows 3–18: Repeat Row 2.

Row 19 and Trim: Sk first vertical bar. Sc in each st across, inserting hook into each st as for Tss. Work 2 or 3 sc in the corner to keep it square, then, working in the row ends and bottom edge of foundation chain, sc down the side, across the bottom, and up other side, working 2 or 3 sc in each corner. Join to first st with sl st.

Fasten off.

Knit Stitch Washcloth

Ch 24.

Row 1: Tss in second ch from hook and in each ch across—24 lps on hook. Return.

Row 2: Sk first vertical bar. *Tks in next vertical bar. Repeat from * across. Return.

Rows 3–27: Repeat Row 2.

Row 28 and Trim: Sk first vertical bar. Sc in each st across, inserting hook into each st as for Tks. Work 2 or 3 sc in the corner to keep it square, then, working in the row ends and bottom edge of foundation chain, sc down the side, across the bottom, and up other side, working 2 or 3 sc in each corner. Join to first st with sl st.

Fasten off.

Knit Stitch Washcloth

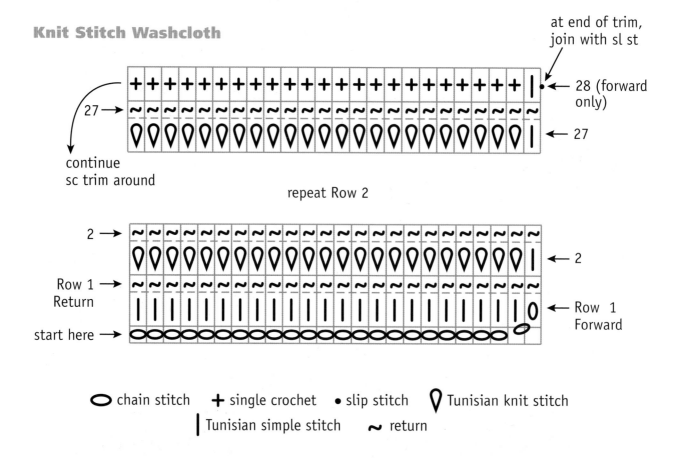

at end of trim,
join with sl st

28 (forward only)

27

continue
sc trim around

repeat Row 2

2

Row 1
Return

start here

2

Row 1
Forward

◯ chain stitch   ✛ single crochet   • slip stitch   ⬯ Tunisian knit stitch

❘ Tunisian simple stitch   ～ return

Little Arches Washcloth

With B, ch 25.

Row 1: Tss in second ch from hook and in each ch across—25 lps on hook. Return, changing to A when 2 lps remain on hook.

NOTE Do not cut yarn when changing colors.

Row 2: Sk first vertical bar. Sl next vertical bar. *Bring yarn to front of hook. Working behind yarn, sl next vertical bar on hook. Bring yarn to back of hook. Working in front of yarn, sl next vertical bar on hook. Repeat from * across to last vertical bar, Tss in last vertical bar—25 lps on hook. Return, changing to B when 2 lps remain on hook.

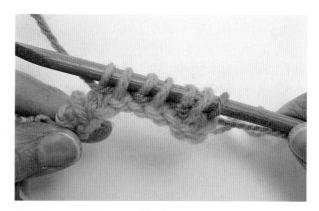

Slipping yarn to front and back

Row 3: Sk first vertical bar. *Insert hook in horizontal bar slightly above and behind next vertical bar, yo, pull up lp. Repeat from * across to last st, Tss in last st—25 lps on hook. Return, changing to A when 2 lps remain on hook.

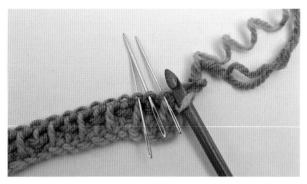

Row 4: Sk first vertical bar. *Bring yarn to front of hook. Sl next vertical bar on hook. Bring yarn to back of hook. Sl next vertical bar on hook. Repeat from * across to last vertical bar, Tss in last vertical bar. Return, changing to B when 2 lps remain on hook.

Needles show positions of next three horizontal bars.

Little Arches Washcloth

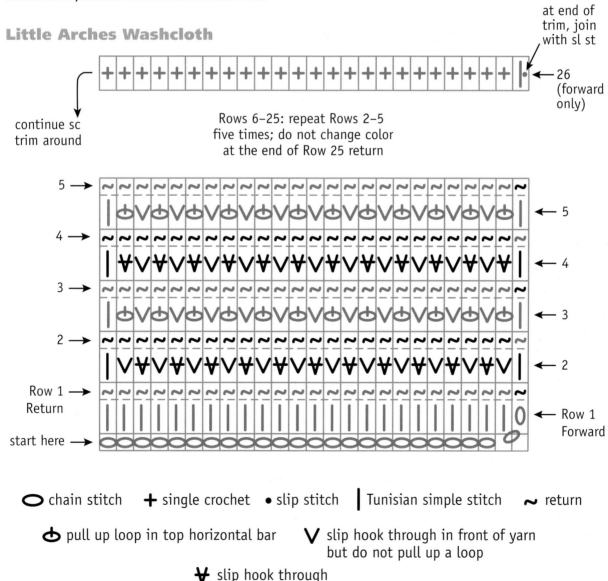

at end of trim, join with sl st

← 26 (forward only)

continue sc trim around

Rows 6–25: repeat Rows 2–5 five times; do not change color at the end of Row 25 return

5 →

← 5

4 →

← 4

3 →

← 3

2 →

← 2

Row 1 Return →

start here →

← Row 1 Forward

O chain stitch **+** single crochet **•** slip stitch **|** Tunisian simple stitch **~** return

♉ pull up loop in top horizontal bar **V** slip hook through in front of yarn but do not pull up a loop

Ѵ slip hook through behind yarn but do not pull up loop

Contrasting yarn is staggered

Row 5: Sk first vertical bar. Pull up lp in horizontal bar
slightly above and behind each vertical bar across to
last st, Tss in last st—25 lps on hook. Return, changing to A when 2 lps remain on hook.

*The needle in this photo shows the horizontal bar to work
into on Row 5.*

Rows 6–25: Repeat Rows 2–5. Do not change to A at the
end of Row 25.

Row 26 and Trim: Sk first vertical bar. Sc in each st
across, inserting hook into each st as for Tss. Work 2
or 3 sc in the corner to keep it square, then, working
in the row ends and bottom edge of foundation
chain, sc down the side, across the bottom, and up
other side, working 2 or 3 sc in each corner. Join to
first st with sl st.

Fasten off.

Checked Washcloth

With A, ch 25.

Row 1: Tss in second ch from hook and in each ch
across—25 lps on hook. Return, changing to B when
2 lps remain on hook. Do not cut A.

> **NOTE** Do not cut yarn when changing colors.
> When changing from one color to another, bring
> the new color over old color.

Row 2: Sk first vertical bar. Sl next vertical bar. *Pull up
lp in horizontal bar above and behind next vertical
bar, sl next vertical bar. Repeat from * across to last
vertical bar, Tss in last vertical bar—25 lps on hook.
Return, changing to A when 2 lps remain on hook.

Working in horizontal bar

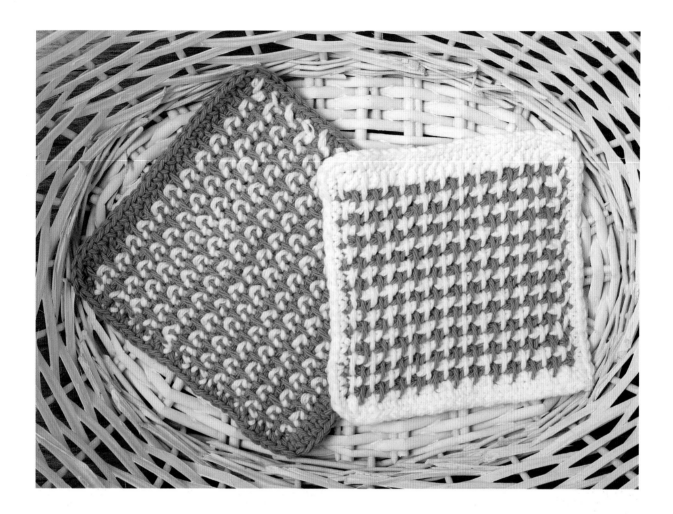

Row 3: Sk first vertical bar. Pull up lp in horizontal bar above and behind next vertical bar. *Sl next vertical bar, pull up lp in horizontal bar above and behind next vertical bar. Repeat from * across to last vertical bar, Tss in last vertical bar—25 lps on hook. Return, changing to B when 2 lps remain on hook.

> **NOTE** Make sure the vertical bars you are slipping onto the hook are from the row below, not from 2 rows below.

Rows 4–21: Repeat Rows 2 and 3. Do not change to B at the end of Row 21.

Row 22 and Trim: Sk first vertical bar. Sc in each st across, inserting hook into each st as for Tss. Work 2 or 3 sc in the corner to keep it square, then, working in the row ends and bottom edge of foundation chain, sc down the side, across the bottom, and up other side, working 2 or 3 sc in each corner. Join to first st with sl st.

Fasten off.

Finishing (all washcloths)

Weave in ends. Lightly steam block on WS.

Checked Washcloth

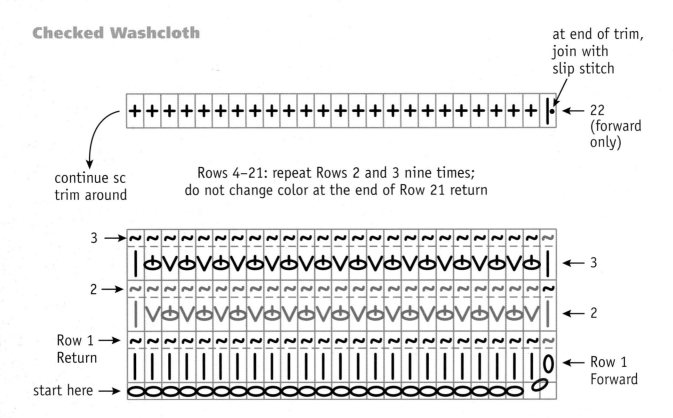

at end of trim,
join with
slip stitch

← 22
(forward
only)

continue sc
trim around

Rows 4–21: repeat Rows 2 and 3 nine times;
do not change color at the end of Row 21 return

3 →

← 3

2 →

← 2

Row 1 →
Return

← Row 1
Forward

start here →

O chain stitch   **+** single crochet   **•** slip stitch   **|** Tunisian simple stitch   **~** return

♉ pull up loop in top horizontal bar   **V** slip hook through stitch
                                              but do not pull up a loop

Harlequin Blanket

Tunisian entrelac makes a big impact using simple geometric shapes. You won't need an extra-long hook extension for this project; the maximum number of loops on the hook at any one time is just seven!

MEASUREMENTS

27½ in. (67 cm) wide by 33 in. (84 cm) long

MATERIALS

Red Heart Classic (100% acrylic; 3.5 oz./100 g,
190 yd./174 m)

Medium

Color A: Yellow (0230), 2 skeins

Color B: White (0001), 1 skein

Color C: Soft Navy (0853), 1 skein

U.S. size J-10 (6.0 mm) Tunisian crochet hook
(or size needed to obtain gauge)

U.S. size J-10 (6.0 mm) regular crochet hook

Tapestry needle

GAUGE

Gauge is flexible for this project. Suggested gauge:
Each entrelac square = 1¼ by 1¼ in. (3 by 3 cm),
blocked. For gauge swatch, ch 33. Work beginning
triangle, two full squares, and ending triangle as
in pattern.

Special Stitch

Make 1 (M1): Insert hook in space before next st, yo,
pull up lp.

Notes

1. The finished blanket will be turned so that the stripes
run vertically and the straight edges are at the top
and bottom.

2. The return passes in entrelac differ from those in
other Tunisian crochet stitch patterns. Each return
pass is: *Yo, pull through 2 lps. Repeat from * until
1 lp remains. It does not start with [yo, pull through
1 lp] as in a standard return pass.

3. The stitch count for the starting and ending triangles
varies on each row of those triangles (it increases in
the starting triangle and decreases in the ending triangle). Each square has 6 stitches per row (7 loops
on hook at end of each forward pass).

4. See page 126 for step-by-step photos and instructions for Make 1.

Pattern

Tier 1

With A and Tunisian crochet hook, ch 123.

STARTING TRIANGLE

Row 1: Tss in second ch from hook—2 lps on hook.
Return.

> **NOTE** Remember that the return pass in this pat-
> tern is different from the standard return pass (see
> Note 2 above).

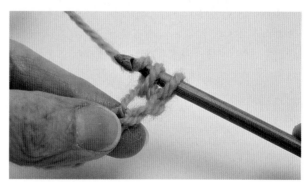

Row 1 return pass of starting triangle

Row 2: M1, Tss in next unworked ch—3 lps on hook. Return.

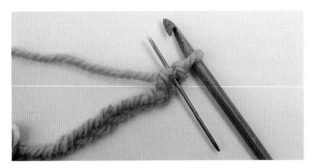

Needle indicates position for M1.

Row 3: M1, Tss in next vertical bar, Tss in next unworked ch—4 lps on hook. Return.

Row 4: M1, Tss in next 2 vertical bars, Tss in next unworked ch—5 lps on hook. Return.

Row 5: M1, Tss in next 3 vertical bars, Tss in next unworked ch—6 lps on hook. Return.

Row 6: M1, Tss in next 4 vertical bars, Tss in next unworked ch—7 lps on hook. Return.

Row 7: Sk first vertical bar. Sl st in next 5 vertical bars, entering each st as for Tss. Sl st into same stitch as final st of Row 6. Do not fasten off—1 lp on hook.

NOTE Row 7 of Tier 1 starting triangle, Row 6 of Tier 1 squares, and Row 6 of Tier 1 ending triangle are forward only. On Tier 2, Row 6 on all squares is forward only. On Tier 3, work forward only on Row 6 of starting triangle, Row 6 of all squares, and Row 6 of ending triangle.

Section of Blanket

Repeat Tiers 2 and 3, working odd-numbered tiers in A, even-numbered tiers alternating C and B. Tier 23 is final tier.

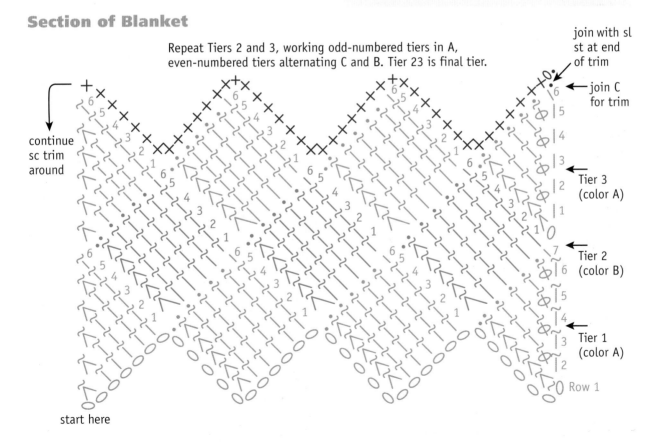

join with sl st at end of trim

join C for trim

Tier 3 (color A)

Tier 2 (color B)

Tier 1 (color A)

continue sc trim around

start here

Row 1

○ chain stitch   + single crochet | Tunisian simple stitch   • slip stitch   ⏀ Make 1

✕✕ single crochet 2 together   ⋀̃ yo, pull through 2 lps on return   ~ return

End of starting triangle

NOTE Keep the sl sts slightly loose; you will work into them on the next tier of blocks.

SQUARE

Row 1: Tss in next 6 unworked chs—7 lps on hook. Return.

Beginning of first square

Rows 2–5: Sk first vertical bar. Tss in next 5 sts, Tss in next unworked ch—7 lps on hook. Return.

Row 6: Sk first vertical bar. Sl st in next 5 vertical bars, entering each st as for Tss. Sl st in same st as final st of Row 5—1 lp on hook.

Repeat Square until 6 unworked chs remain. You will use these for the Ending Triangle.

ENDING TRIANGLE

Row 1: Tss in next 6 unworked chs—7 lps on hook. Return.

Row 2: Sk first vertical bar. Tss in next 5 sts—6 lps on hook. Return.

Row 3: Sk first vertical bar. Tss in next 4 sts—5 lps on hook. Return.

Row 4: Sk first vertical bar. Tss in next 3 sts—4 lps on hook. Return.

Row 5: Sk first vertical bar. Tss in next 2 sts—3 lps on hook. Return.

Row 6: Sk first vertical bar. Tss in next st. Return. Fasten off.

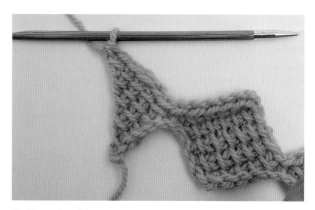

Ending triangle

Tier 2

FIRST SQUARE

With RS facing, join B in top right corner of starting triangle of previous tier (counts as 1 lp).

Row 1: Tss in next 5 sl sts. Insert hook in side edge of Row 1 of first square, yo, pull up lp—7 lps on hook. Return.

Rows 2–5: Sk first vertical bar. Tss in next 5 sts, Tss in end stitch on next row of square from previous tier—7 lps on hook. Return.

Row 6: Sk first vertical bar. Sl st in next 5 vertical bars, entering each st as for Tss. Sl st in same st as final st of Row 5—1 lp on hook.

SECOND AND FOLLOWING SQUARES

Row 1: Tss in next 5 sl sts (on second side of first square from previous tier). Insert hook in side edge of Row 1 of next square from previous tier, yo, pull up lp—7 lps on hook. Return.

Rows 2–5: Sk first vertical bar. Tss in next 5 sts, Tss in last stitch of next row of square from previous tier—7 lps on hook. Return.

Row 6: Sk first vertical bar. Sl st in next 5 vertical bars, entering each st as for Tss. Sl st in same st as final st of Row 5—1 lp on hook.

Repeat Rows 1–6 across. Each block on this tier is a square; no ending triangle is needed. Work final sl stitch into point of ending triangle of Tier 1. Fasten off.

Tier 3

STARTING TRIANGLE

With RS facing, join A at base of first st in first square of previous tier.

Row 1: Ch 2. Tss in second ch from hook, insert hook in side of Row 1 in first square from previous tier, yo, pull up lp—3 lps on hook. Return.

Row 2: M1, Tss in next vertical bar, Tss in next st of square of previous tier—4 lps on hook. Return.

Row 3: M1, Tss in next 2 vertical bars, Tss in next st of square of previous tier—5 lps on hook. Return.

Row 4: M1, Tss in next 3 vertical bars, Tss in next st of square of previous tier—6 lps on hook. Return.

Row 5: M1, Tss in next 4 vertical bars, Tss in next st of square of previous tier—7 lps on hook. Return.

Row 6: Sk first vertical bar. Sl st in next 5 vertical bars, entering each st as for Tss. Sl st into same stitch as final st of Row 6—1 lp on hook.

SQUARES

Work as for squares of Tier 2.

ENDING TRIANGLE

Row 1: Tss in next 6 sl sts of previous tier—7 lps on hook. Return.

Row 2: Sk first vertical bar. Tss in next 5 sts—6 lps on hook. Return.

Row 3: Sk first vertical bar. Tss in next 4 sts—5 lps on hook. Return.

Row 4: Sk first vertical bar. Tss in next 3 sts—4 lps on hook. Return.

Row 5: Sk first vertical bar. Tss in next 2 sts—3 lps on hook. Return.

Row 6: Sk first vertical bar. Tss in next st. Return. Fasten off.

Tiers 4–23

Repeat Tiers 2 and 3, working all odd-numbered tiers in A and alternating between C and B for even-numbered tiers. Tier 23, the final tier, is the twelfth tier in color A.

Trim and Finishing

Weave in ends. Lightly steam block on wrong side. With RS facing, join C in any corner. Ch 1. Sc all around blanket. On the zigzag edges, work 3 sc at the point of each diamond, and sc2tog where two diamonds meet. Sl st to beg ch. Fasten off.

Weave in remaining ends. Lightly steam block trim on WS if necessary.

Thumbless Mittens

SKILL LEVEL

EASY

Thumbless mittens are quick to crochet and will keep your little one's hands cozy and warm. Hook several pairs in a rainbow of colors for a memorable shower gift.

MEASUREMENTS

One size fits 0–6 months, to fit hand circumference up to 6 in. (15 cm). Length is 5¼ in. (13.3 cm)

MATERIALS

Plymouth Yarn Encore (75% acrylic, 25% wool; 3.5 oz./100 g, 200 yd./183 m)

Medium

Miami Aqua (0235), 1 skein

U.S. size H-8 (5.0 mm) Tunisian crochet hook (or size needed to obtain gauge)

Tapestry needle

GAUGE

First 9 rows of pattern (24 sts and 9 rows) = 5½ in. (14 cm) wide by 2¼ in. (5.75 cm) high, unblocked

Special Stitches

Make 1 (M1): Insert hook from front to back in space before next st, yo, pull up lp—1 st increased.

Tunisian knit stitch 2 together (Tks2tog): Insert hook through next 2 sts at same time, with hook ending at back of work as for Tks. Yo, pull up lp—1 st decreased.

Note

See pages 126 and 131 for step-by-step photos and instructions for Make 1 and Tunisian knit stitch 2 together.

Pattern

Ch 24.

Row 1 (RS): Tps in second ch from hook and in next chain. *Tks in next 2 chs, Tps in next 2 chs. Repeat from * across until 1 ch remains. Insert hook in final ch, yo, pull up lp—24 lps on hook. Return.

Row 2: Sk first vertical bar. *Tps in next 2 sts, Tks in next 2 sts. Repeat from * across until 1 st remains. Tks in final st. Return.

Rows 3–9: Repeat Row 2.

Row 10 (increase row): Sk first vertical bar. Tks in next 4 sts, M1, [Tks in next 8 sts, M1] twice, Tks in remaining 3 sts—27 lps on hook. Return.

Row 11: Sk first vertical bar. Tks in each st across—27 lps on hook. Return.

Rows 12–21: Repeat Row 11.

Row 22 (begin shaping): Sk first vertical bar. *Tks2tog, Tks in next 2 sts. Repeat from * across until 2 sts remain. Tks in last 2 sts—21 lps on hook. Return.

Row 23: Sk first vertical bar. Tks in each st across—21 lps on hook. Return.

Row 24: Sk first vertical bar. *Tks2tog, Tks in next 2 sts. Repeat from * across—16 lps on hook. Return.

Row 25: Sk first vertical bar. Tks in each st across—16 lps on hook. Return.

Row 26: Sk first vertical bar. *Tks2tog, Tks in next 2 sts. Repeat from * across until 3 sts remain. Tks2tog, Tks in final st—12 lps on hook. Return.

Row 27: Sk first vertical bar. Sc in each st across, inserting hook into each st as for Tks—11 sc. Fasten off, leaving a long tail.

Finishing

With WS facing, thread tail onto tapestry needle. Sew top of mitten and side seam closed. Weave in ends. Lightly steam block if desired.

Mittens

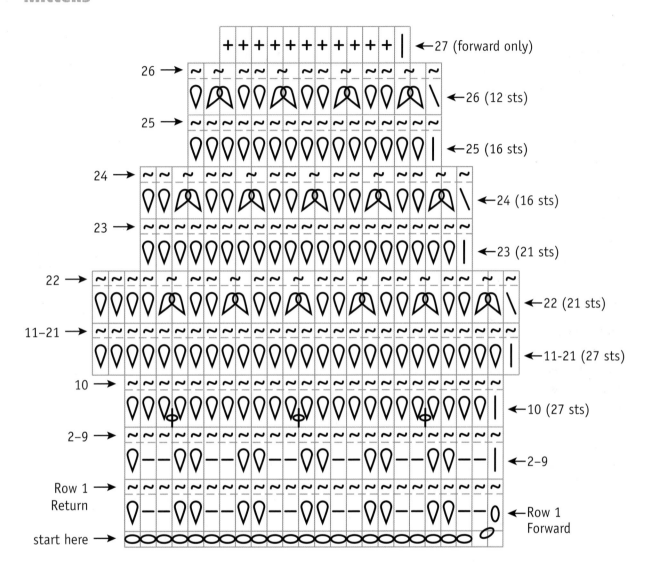

27 (forward only)

26 → 26 (12 sts)

25 → 25 (16 sts)

24 → 24 (16 sts)

23 → 23 (21 sts)

22 → 22 (21 sts)

11–21 → 11–21 (27 sts)

10 → 10 (27 sts)

2–9 → 2–9

Row 1 Return → Row 1 Forward

start here →

+ single crochet   — Tunisian purl stitch   ⏀ Tunisian full stitch (make 1)   ~ return

⋁ Tunisian knit stitch   ⋀ Tunisian knit stitch 2 together   ◯ chain stitch

Zippered Hoodie

SKILL LEVEL

INTERMEDIATE

Black and white can be sophisticated, but the loop trim that frames the hood of this zippered sweater makes these high-contrast colors pop with fun. Play "let's pretend" with your little panda, penguin, or zebra when he or she wears this comfortable garment.

MEASUREMENTS

Instructions are for size 6–9 months, with size 12 months in parentheses

MATERIALS

Plymouth Select DK Merino Superwash (100% superwash fine merino wool; 1.75 oz./50 g, 130 yd./119 m)

3

Light

Color A: Black (1050), 3 (4) skeins

Color B: White (1000), 4 (5) skeins

U.S. size H-8 (5.0 mm) Tunisian crochet hook (or size needed to obtain gauge)

U.S. size F-5 (3.75 mm) regular crochet hook (or size needed to keep trim flat)

Separating zipper, black, 10 in. (25 cm) long

Straight pins

Sewing needle

Black sewing thread for attaching zipper

Tapestry needle

GAUGE

20 sts and 21 rows in Tks = 4 in. (10.2 cm), blocked

Special Stitches

Loop Stitch (LS): Insert hook into stitch as for sc. Using a finger of your free hand, pull up the yarn to form a loop approximately 1 in. (2.5 cm) tall. Put hook behind both both strands of the loop near the base and pull up both strands, leaving the loopy end sticking out the back. Release lp from your finger. Using working yarn (not tall lp), yo, pull through all lps.

Make 1 (M1): Insert hook from front to back in space before next vertical bar, yo, pull up lp.

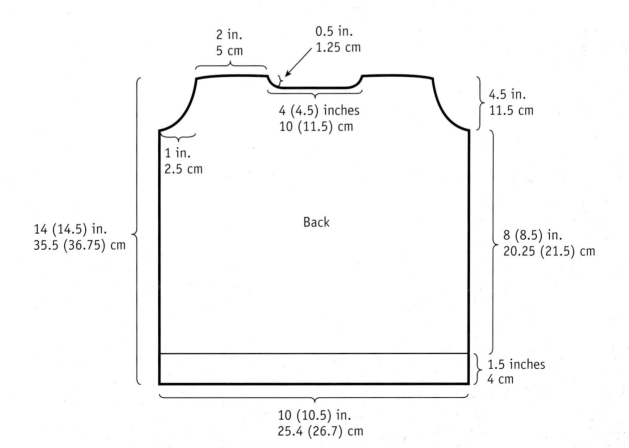

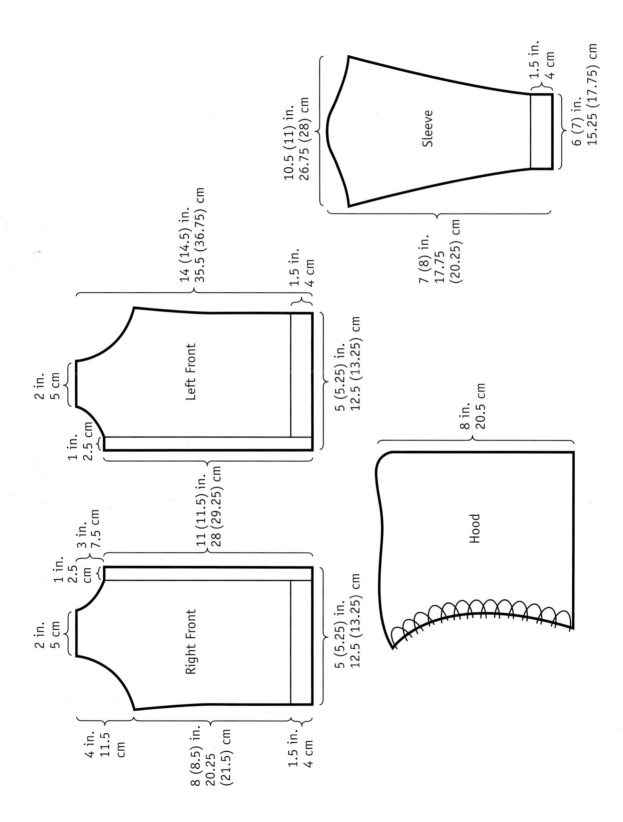

Sleeve

10.5 (11) in.
26.75 (28) cm

1.5 in.
4 cm

6 (7) in.
15.25 (17.75) cm

7 (8) in.
17.75 (20.25) cm

14 (14.5) in.
35.5 (36.75) cm

Left Front

1.5 in.
4 cm

2 in.
5 cm

1 in.
2.5 cm

5 (5.25) in.
12.5 (13.25) cm

11 (11.5) in.
28 (29.25) cm

Right Front

3 in.
7.5 cm

1 in.
2.5 cm

2 in.
5 cm

5 (5.25) in.
12.5 (13.25) cm

4 in.
11.5 cm

8 (8.5) in.
20.25 (21.5) cm

1.5 in.
4 cm

Hood

8 in.
20.5 cm

Notes

1. See pages 125 and 126 for step-by-step photos and instructions for working loop stitch and Make 1.
2. In the pattern, the loop stitch is worked with two yarns held together. If you are new to this stitch, practice with a single yarn first.

Pattern

Back

With A, ch 48 (52).

Row 1 (RS): Tps in second ch from hook and in next ch. *Tks in next 2 chs, Tps in next 2 chs. Repeat from * across until 1 ch remains. Tks in last ch—48 (52) lps on hook. Return.

Row 2: Sk first vertical bar. *Tps in next 2 sts, Tks in next 2 sts. Repeat from * across until 3 sts remain. Tps in next 2 sts, Tks in final st—48 (52) lps on hook. Return.

Rows 3–6: Repeat Row 2. Change to B when 2 lps remain on hook at end of Row 6 Return.

Rows 7–48 (7–50): Sk first vertical bar. Tks in each st across—48 (52) lps on hook. Return.

ARMHOLE SHAPING

Row 49 (51): Sk first vertical bar. Sl st in next 4 sts, inserting hook into each st as for Tks. Tks in each st across, leaving final 4 sts unworked—40 (44) lps on hook. Return.

Rows 50–71 (52–75): Sk first vertical bar. Tks in each st across—40 (44) lps on hook. Return.

RIGHT SIDE OF BACK NECKLINE SHAPING

Row 72 (76): Sk first vertical bar. Tks in next 12 sts—13 lps on hook.

Return: [Yo, pull through 2 lps] until 1 lp remains on hook.

NOTE This return differs from standard return.

Row 73 (77): Sk first vertical bar. Tks in next 11 sts—12 lps on hook. Return (resume standard returns).

Rows 74–75 (78–79): Sk first vertical bar. Tks in each st across—12 lps on hook. Return.

Row 76 (80): Sk first vertical bar. Sc in each st across, inserting hook in each st as for Tks—11 sc. Fasten off.

LEFT SIDE OF BACK NECKLINE SHAPING

Row 72 (76): Skip first 14 (18) sts after the sts of Row 72 (76) of Right Side of Back Neckline Shaping. Join yarn in next st, pull up lp. Tks in each remaining st, ending at armhole edge—13 lps on hook. Return.

Row 73 (77): Sk first vertical bar. Sl st in next st, inserting hook into st as for Tks. Tks in each remaining st—12 lps on hook. Return.

Rows 74–75 (78–79): Sk first vertical bar. Tks in each st across—12 lps on hook. Return.

Row 76 (80): Sk first vertical bar. Sc in each stitch across, inserting hook into sts as for Tks—11 sc. Fasten off.

Back

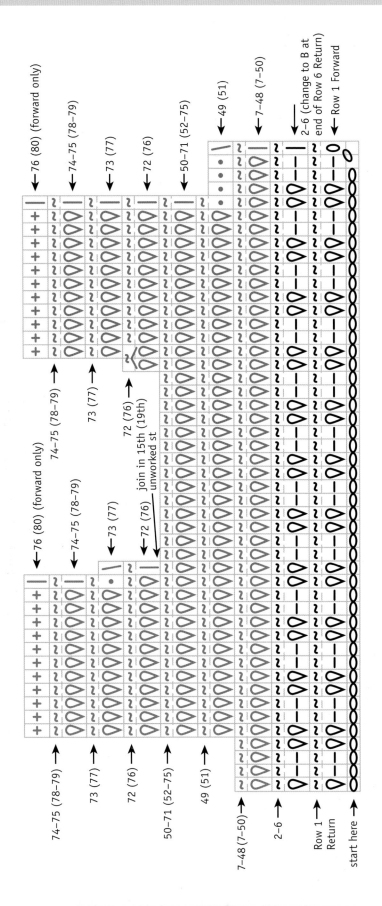

76 (80) (forward only)

74–75 (78–79)

73 (77)

72 (76)

50–71 (52–75)

49 (51)

7–48 (7–50)

2–6 (change to B at end of Row 6 Return)

Row 1 Forward

76 (80) (forward only)

74–75 (78–79)

73 (77)

72 (76)

join in 15th (19th) unworked st

74–75 (78–79)

73 (77)

72 (76)

50–71 (52–75)

49 (51)

7–48 (7–50)

2–6

Row 1 Return

start here

○ chain stitch — Tunisian purl stitch • slip stitch

+ single crochet

Ɛ 2 stitches together

≀ Tunisian simple stitch

◊ Tunisian knit stitch

Ɛ close (return)

≀ return

Front Left

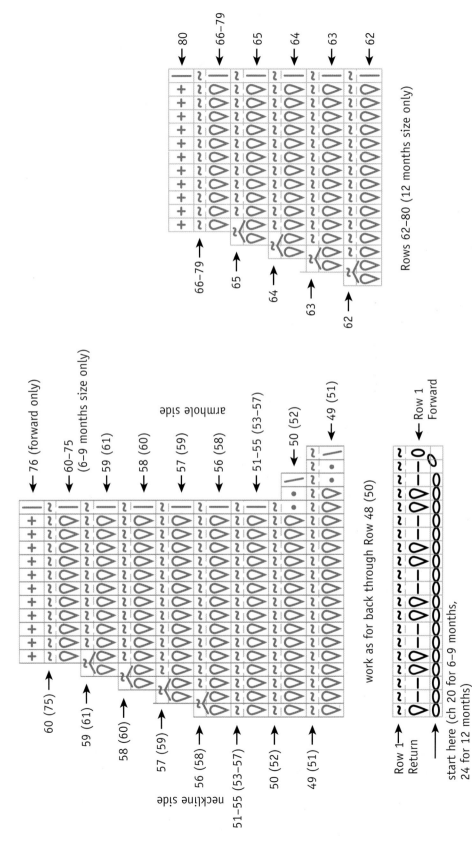

Rows 62–80 (12 months size only)

80
66–79
65
64
63
62

76 (forward only)
60–75 (6–9 months size only)
59 (61)
58 (60)
57 (59)
56 (58)
51–55 (53–57)
50 (52)
49 (51)

armhole side

neckline side

60 (75)
59 (61)
58 (60)
57 (59)
56 (58)
51–55 (53–57)
50 (52)
49 (51)

work as for back through Row 48 (50)

Row 1 Forward

Row 1 Return

start here (ch 20 for 6–9 months, 24 for 12 months)

O chain stitch — Tunisian purl stitch ♀ Tunisian knit stitch ‿ return

+ single crochet • slip stitch ⟨ close (return) 2 stitches together | Tunisian simple stitch

Front Left

With A, ch 20 (24).

Rows 1–48 (1–50): Work as for back—20 (24) lps on hook at end of each forward pass.

ARMHOLE SHAPING

Row 49 (51): Sk first vertical bar. Sl st in next 2 sts, inserting hook into each st as for Tks. Tks in each remaining st—18 (22) lps on hook. Return.

Row 50 (52): Sk first vertical bar. Sl st in next 2 sts, inserting hook into each st as for Tks. Tks in each remaining st—16 (20) lps. Return.

Rows 51–55 (53–57): Sk first vertical bar. Tks in each st across—16 (20) lps on hook. Return.

NECKLINE SHAPING

Row 56 (58): Sk first vertical bar. Tks in each st across—16 (20) lps on hook.

Return: *Yo, pull through 2 lps. Repeat from * until 1 lp remains on hook.

NOTE This return differs from standard return.

Row 57 (59): Sk first vertical bar. Tks in each st across—15 (19) lps on hook. Return as for Row 56 (58).

Row 58 (60): Sk first vertical bar. Tks in each lp across—14 (18) lps on hook. Return as for Row 56 (58).

Row 59 (61): Sk first vertical bar. Tks in each lp across—13 (17) lps on hook. Return as for Row 56 (58).

6–9 Months Size Only

Row 60: Sk first vertical bar. Tks in each lp across—12 (16) lps on hook. Return.

NOTE Standard returns resume with Row 60.

Rows 61–75: Sk first vertical bar. Tks in each lp across—12 lps on hook. Return.

Row 76: Sk first vertical bar. Sc in each stitch across, inserting hook in each st as for Tks—11 sc. Fasten off.

12 Months Size Only

Row 62: Sk first vertical bar. Tks in each lp across—16 lps on hook. Return as for Row 58.

Row 63: Sk first vertical bar. Tks in each lp across—15 lps on hook. Return as for Row 58.

Row 64: Sk first vertical bar. Tks in each lp across—14 lps on hook. Return as for Row 58.

Row 65: Sk first vertical bar. Tks in each lp across—13 lps on hook. Return as for Row 58.

Row 66: Sk first vertical bar. Tks in each st across—12 lps on hook. Return.

NOTE Standard returns resume with Row 66.

Rows 67–79: Sk first vertical bar. Tks in each st across—12 lps on hook. Return.

Row 80: Sk first vertical bar. Sc in each stitch across, inserting hook in each st as for Tks—11 sc. Fasten off.

Front Right

With A, ch 20 (24).

Rows 1–48 (1–50): Work as for back—20 (24) lps on hook at end of each forward pass.

ARMHOLE SHAPING

Row 49 (51): Sk first vertical bar. Tks in each st across, leaving last 2 sts unworked—18 (22) lps on hook. Return.

Row 50 (52): Sk first vertical bar. Tks in each st across, leaving last 2 sts unworked—16 (20) lps on hook. Return.

Rows 51–55 (53–57): Sk first vertical bar. Tks in each st across—16 (20) lps on hook. Return.

NECKLINE SHAPING

Row 56 (58): Sk first vertical bar. Sl st in next st, inserting hook into st as for Tks. Tks in each remaining st across—15 (19) lps on hook. Return.

Row 57 (59): Sk first vertical bar. Sl st in next st, inserting hook into st as for Tks. Tks in each remaining st across—14 (18) lps on hook. Return.

Row 58 (60): Sk first vertical bar. Sl st in next st, inserting hook into st as for Tks. Tks in each remaining st across—13 (17) lps on hook. Return.

Front Right

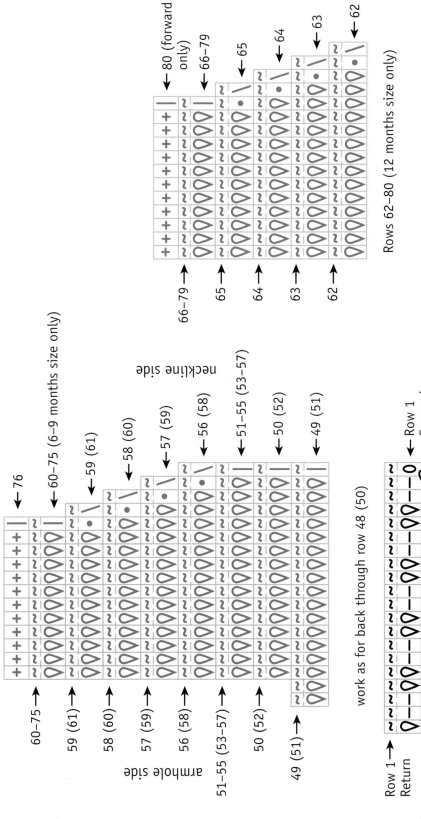

76

60–75 (6–9 months size only)

59 (61)

58 (60)

57 (59)

56 (58)

51–55 (53–57)

50 (52)

49 (51)

60–75 →

59 (61) →

58 (60) →

57 (59) →

56 (58) →

51–55 (53–57) →

50 (52) →

49 (51) →

armhole side

neckline side

80 (forward only)

66–79

65

64

63

62

66–79 →

65 →

64 →

63 →

62 →

Rows 62–80 (12 months size only)

work as for back through row 48 (50)

Row 1 Forward

Row 1 Return →

start here (ch 20 for 6–9 months, 24 for 12 months)

⌀ chain stitch   — Tunisian purl stitch   ∫ return

+ single crochet   • slip stitch

∩ Tunisian knit stitch | Tunisian simple stitch

Row 59 (61): Sk first vertical bar. Sl st in next st, inserting hook into st as for Tks. Tks in each remaining st across—12 (16) lps on hook. Return.

6–9 Months Size Only

Rows 60–75: Sk first vertical bar. Tks in each st across—12 lps on hook. Return.

Row 76: Sk first vertical bar. Sc in each stitch across, inserting hook in each st as for Tks—11 sc. Fasten off.

12 Months Size Only

Row 62: Sk first vertical bar. Sl st in next st, inserting hook into st as for Tks. Tks in each remaining st across—15 lps on hook. Return.

Row 63: Sk first vertical bar. Sl st in next st, inserting hook into st as for Tks. Tks in each remaining st across—14 lps on hook. Return.

Row 64: Sk first vertical bar. Sl st in next st, inserting hook into st as for Tks. Tks in each remaining st across—13 lps on hook. Return.

Row 65: Sk first vertical bar. Sl st in next st, inserting hook into st as for Tks. Tks in each remaining st across—12 lps on hook. Return.

Rows 66–79: Sk first vertical bar. Tks in each st across—12 lps on hook. Return.

Row 80: Sk first vertical bar. Sc in each stitch across, inserting hook in each st as for Tks—11 sc. Fasten off.

Sleeve (make 2)

NOTE The sleeve is worked the same way for both sizes through Row 37.

With B, ch 32.

Row 1 (RS): Tps in second ch from hook and in next ch. *Tks in next 2 chs, Tps in next 2 chs. Repeat from * across until 1 ch remains. Tks in final ch—32 lps on hook. Return.

Row 2: Sk first vertical bar. *Tps in next 2 sts, Tks in next 2 sts. Repeat from * across until 3 sts remain. Tps in next 2 sts, Tks in final st—32 lps on hook. Return.

Rows 3–6: Repeat Row 2. Change to A when 2 lps remain on hook at end of Row 6 Return.

Rows 7–10: Sk first vertical bar. Tks in each st across—32 lps on hook. Return.

Row 11: Sk first vertical bar. M1. Tks in each st across until 1 st remains, M1, Tks in final st—34 lps on hook. Return.

Rows 12–14: Sk first vertical bar. Tks in each st across—34 lps on hook. Return.

Row 15: Sk first vertical bar. M1. Tks in each st across until 1 st remains, M1, Tks in final st—36 lps on hook. Return.

Rows 16–18: Sk first vertical bar. Tks in each st across—36 lps on hook. Return.

Row 19: Sk first vertical bar. M1. Tks in each st across until 1 st remains, M1, Tks in final st—38 lps on hook. Return.

Rows 20–22: Sk first vertical bar. Tks in each st across—38 lps on hook. Return.

Row 23: Sk first vertical bar. M1. Tks in each st across until 1 st remains, M1, Tks in final st—40 lps on hook. Return.

Rows 24–26: Sk first vertical bar. Tks in each st across—40 lps on hook. Return.

Row 27: Sk first vertical bar. M1. Tks in each st across until 1 st remains, M1, Tks in final st—42 lps on hook. Return.

Rows 28–30: Sk first vertical bar. Tks in each st across—42 lps on hook. Return.

Row 31: Sk first vertical bar. M1. Tks in each st across until 1 st remains, M1, Tks in final st—44 lps on hook. Return.

Row 32: Sk first vertical bar. Tks in each st across—44 lps on hook. Return.

Row 33: Sk first vertical bar. M1. Tks in each st across until 1 st remains, M1, Tks in final st—46 lps on hook. Return.

Row 34: Sk first vertical bar. Tks in each st across—46 lps on hook. Return.

Row 35: Sk first vertical bar. M1. Tks in each st across until 1 st remains, M1, Tks in final st—48 lps on hook. Return.

Row 36: Sk first vertical bar. Tks in each st across—48 lps on hook. Return.

Sleeve

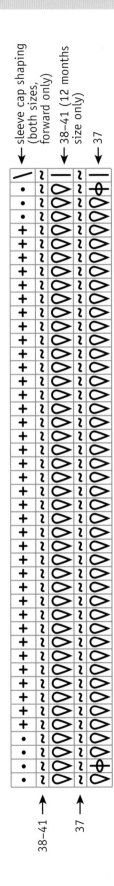

38-41 →

37 →

increase as on Rows 15, 19, 23, 27,
31, 33, 35, and 37 (50 sts in Row 37)

sleeve cap shaping
(both sizes,
forward only)

38-41 (12 months
size only)

37

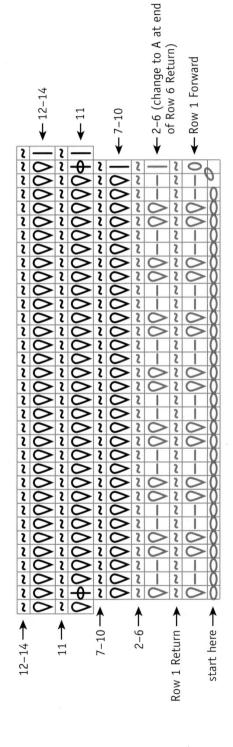

12-14 →

11 →

7-10 →

2-6 →

Row 1 Return →

start here →

12-14

11

7-10

2-6 (change to A at end
of Row 6 Return)

Row 1 Forward

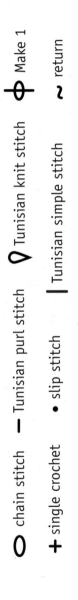

O chain stitch   — Tunisian purl stitch   ⊕ Make 1

V Tunisian knit stitch   ʅ return

| Tunisian simple stitch

+ single crochet   • slip stitch

Row 37: Sk first vertical bar. M1. Tks in each st across until 1 st remains, M1, Tks in final st—50 lps on hook. Return.

> **NOTE** For 6–9 months size, skip to "Sleeve Cap Shaping." For 12 months size, follow instructions for Rows 38–41, then continue with "Sleeve Cap Shaping."

12 Months Size Only

Rows 38–41: Sk first vertical bar. Tks in each st across— 50 lps on hook. Return.

SLEEVE CAP SHAPING

Row 1: Sk first vertical bar. Sl st in next 3 sts, inserting hook into each st as for Tks. Sc across, inserting hook into each st as for Tks, until 4 sts remain. Sl st in final 4 sts, inserting hook into each st as for Tks—4 sl st. Fasten off.

Assembly and Finishing

Weave in ends. Gently steam block all pieces on WS if desired. Sew shoulder seams.

HOOD

Row 1: With RS facing, join A at right front neckline. Tks in each st across right front, back, and left front. Return.

Row 2: Sk first vertical bar. Tks in each st across. Return.

Repeat Row 2 until hood measures approximately 8 in. (20.5 cm) from bottom edge.

With WS facing, bring edges of hood together to form top. Sew seam.

SLEEVES

With WS facing, sew sleeves to body. Sew sleeve seams.

FRONT TRIM

> **NOTE** The fronts each have 5 rows of sc trim; the hood has 2 rows. The loop trim is added to the hood afterwards.

Row 1: With RS facing, join A at bottom corner of right front (very first row of ribbing). Using regular crochet hook, sc in each st up right front, around hood, and down left front.

Row 2: Ch 1, turn. Sc in each st up left side of front, around hood, and down right side of front.

Row 3: Ch 1, turn. Sc in each st up right side of front. Do not continue around hood.

Row 4: Ch 1, turn. Sc in each st down right side of front.

Row 5: Repeat Row 3. Fasten off.

FINISH LEFT SIDE OF FRONT

Row 3: With RS facing, join B where left top neckline meets hood. Sc in each st down left front.

Row 4: Ch 1, turn. Sc in each st up left side of front.

Row 5: Ch 1, turn. Sc in each st down left side of front. Fasten off.

Hood

repeat Row 2 until work measures 8 in. (20.5 cm);
with WS facing, sew top seam

2

Row 1 Forward

with RS facing join at
right-hand side of front

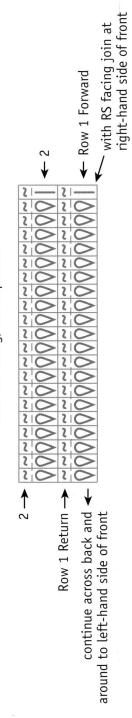

2

Row 1 Return

continue across back and
around to left-hand side of front

| Tunisian simple stitch   ᓇ Tunisian knit stitch   ᘔ return

Front Trim

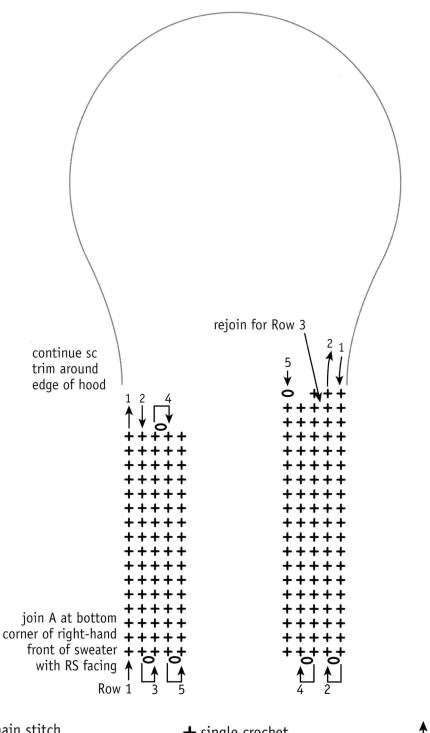

rejoin for Row 3

continue sc
trim around
edge of hood

join A at bottom
corner of right-hand
front of sweater
with RS facing

Row 1

O chain stitch   **+** single crochet   ↑ turn

Loop Trim

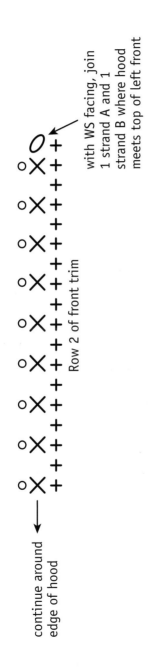

continue around
edge of hood

Row 2 of front trim

with WS facing, join
1 strand A and 1
strand B where hood
meets top of left front

0 chain stitch

+ single crochet

X̥ loop stitch

LOOP TRIM

With WS facing, join 1 strand A and 1 strand B held together where hood meets top of left front. Using Tunisian hook size H as a regular crochet hook, ch 1. *Work 1 LS in next st, skip next st. Repeat from * around hood to other end. Fasten off.

Weave in any remaining ends.

> NOTE The loop stitches are worked on the WS because the loops form on the back of the work. Working them on the WS means they will be visible on the RS; this also keeps them away from the baby's face.

INSTALL ZIPPER

> NOTE This is one method for zipper installation. If you prefer a different technique, or can do this competently on a sewing machine, use whatever method suits you best.

With zipper closed, place it faceup on a table with the edges of the sweater on top, RS up. Pin the zipper in place, making sure the rows on each side line up properly. Baste the zipper to the sweater, then remove pins. With WS facing, backstitch through the sweater and the zipper, as close to the teeth as possible. Remove the basting thread as you go. Check periodically to make sure the sides of the zipper line up. Fold back excess fabric at top of zipper so it is hidden by front of sweater; sew in place.

Favorite Skirt

SKILL LEVEL

INTERMEDIATE

Marguerite stitch, a regular crochet stitch with a floral look, is combined with rows of Tunisian simple stitch in this swingy purple skirt. An elastic waist extends the fit range for each size.

MEASUREMENTS

Instructions are for size 3 months with sizes 6 and 12 months in parentheses

MATERIALS

Crystal Palace Yarns Cuddles (100% acrylic; 1.75 oz./50 g; 98 yd./90 m)

Bulky

Color: Violet (6113), 3 skeins

Size J-10 (6.0 mm) Tunisian crochet hook (or size needed to obtain gauge)

30 in. (76 cm) of non-roll elastic, 1 in. (2.5 cm) wide

Tapestry needle

Sewing thread to match color of yarn

Sewing needle

Safety pin

GAUGE

14 sts and 10 rows in pattern = 4 in. (10 cm), blocked

Note

See page 127 for step-by-step photos and instructions for working the marguerite stitch used in Row 3.

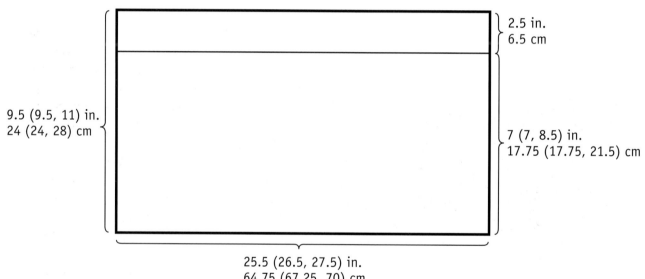

9.5 (9.5, 11) in.
24 (24, 28) cm

2.5 in.
6.5 cm

7 (7, 8.5) in.
17.75 (17.75, 21.5) cm

25.5 (26.5, 27.5) in.
64.75 (67.25, 70) cm

Note: garment is crocheted in one piece then seamed up the back

Pattern

Ch 83 (87, 91).

Row 1: Tss in second ch from hook and in each ch across—83 (87, 91) lps on hook. Return.

Row 2: Sk first vertical bar. Tss in each st across—83 (87, 91) lps on hook. Return.

Row 3 (regular crochet): Ch 2. Insert hook in second ch from hook, yo, pull up lp. Pull up lp in first vertical bar and in next 2 vertical bars (5 lps on hook); yo, pull through all 5 lps, ch 1. *Insert hook in "eye" of flower just made, yo, pull up lp; pull up lp in last vertical bar of flower just made; pull up lp in next 2 vertical bars; yo, pull through all 5 lps on hook, ch 1. Repeat from * across.

Row 4 (regular crochet): Turn. Ch 1 (together with ch from end of Row 3, counts as first hdc), hdc in first flower eye (at the very edge of the row below). *Work 2 hdc in next eye. Repeat from * across, hdc in top of turning ch, ch 1.

The piece after Row 4.

Row 5 (Tunisian crochet): Turn. Sk first hdc. *Tss in next hdc and each hdc across, entering each stitch under top 2 loops of hdc, Tss in beg ch-1 of Row 4—You should have the same number of lps as in the starting ch. Return.

Row 6 (Tunisian crochet): Sk first vertical bar. Tss in each st across. Return.

Rows 7–18 (18, 22): Work Rows 3–6 three (three, four) more times.

NOTE Rows 17–18 (17–18, 21–22) start the casing for the elastic. The following 6 rows finish the casing.

Rows 19–23 (19–23, 23–27): Sk first vertical bar. Tss in each st across—83 (87, 91) lps on hook. Return.

Row 24 (24, 28): Sk first vertical bar. Sc in each st across, inserting hook into each st as for Tss—82 (86, 90) sc. Fasten off.

Finishing

Gently steam block on WS. With tapestry needle, weave in ends.

With WS facing you, use sewing needle and matching thread to sew the back seam, starting at the bottom and stopping where the casing for the elastic begins.

WAIST SEAM AND ELASTIC

Cut elastic 2 in. (5 cm) longer than waist size. The extra length will be used for adjusting fit and finishing the ends. With skirt inside out, fold casing down so the final row matches up with the first Tss row. Using a sewing needle and matching thread, sew the casing together along the bottom edge all around. Do not sew the opening at the side seams.

Pin one end of the elastic to the skirt at side seam opening so it does not get lost in the casing. Feed the elastic through casing. To make this easier, you can attach a safety pin to the end. When the elastic is all the way through, carefully unpin the first end from the skirt and pin the ends together.

Check fit if possible and adjust length of elastic as necessary. (The final amount of elastic used will be anywhere from 2–5 in. [5–12.7 cm] smaller than the waist, whatever is comfortable for the child.) Cut excess, leaving an extra 1 in. (2.5 cm) on each end. Overlap ends of elastic and stitch together firmly. Check fit one more time.

Stitch seam opening closed to completely hide elastic. Turn skirt right side out.

Section of Pattern

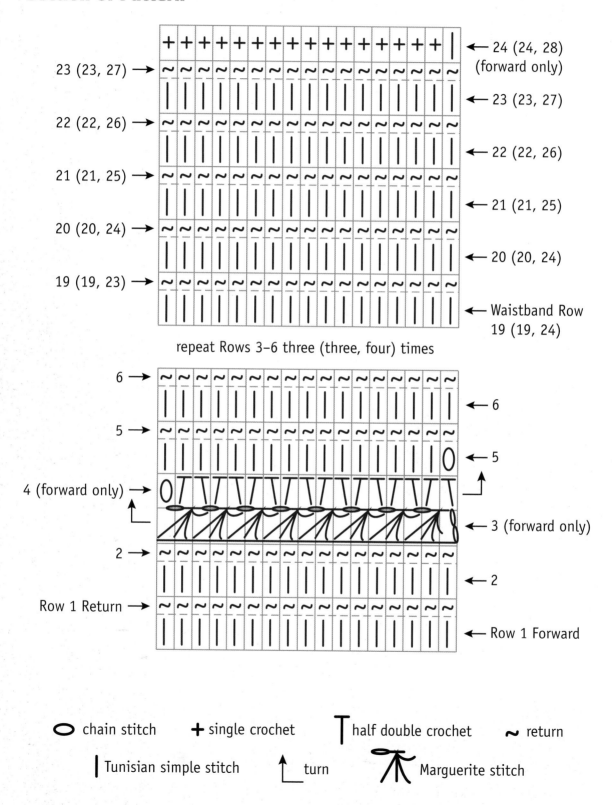

23 (23, 27) →

22 (22, 26) →

21 (21, 25) →

20 (20, 24) →

19 (19, 23) →

← 24 (24, 28) (forward only)

← 23 (23, 27)

← 22 (22, 26)

← 21 (21, 25)

← 20 (20, 24)

← Waistband Row 19 (19, 24)

repeat Rows 3–6 three (three, four) times

6 →

5 →

4 (forward only) →

2 →

Row 1 Return →

← 6

← 5

← 3 (forward only)

← 2

← Row 1 Forward

O chain stitch   **+** single crochet   T half double crochet   **~** return

| Tunisian simple stitch   ↑ turn   Marguerite stitch

Spring Poncho and Turban

Crochet a fresh palette of pinks and greens in this sweet little turban and two-panel poncho.

MEASUREMENTS

Poncho: 11 in. (28 cm) along diagonal from bottom point to top of shoulder, 6.5 in. (16.5 cm) from neck to top of shoulder

Hat circumference: 14 in. (35.5 cm)

MATERIALS

Crystal Palace Cuddles DK (100% microfiber acrylic; 1.7 oz./50 g, 131 yd./120 m)

Light

Color A: Moss Roses (2004), 2 skeins
Color B: Creole Rose (0106), 2 skeins

NOTE Yarn amounts given here are sufficient for both projects.

U.S. size J-10 (6.0 mm) Tunisian crochet hook (or size needed to obtain gauge)
U.S. size H-8 (5.0 mm) regular crochet hook (or size needed to keep border flat)
Tapestry needle

GAUGE

Gauge is flexible for this project. Suggested gauge is 15 sts and 13 rows in pattern = 4 in. (10.2 cm), blocked.

Special Stitches

Tunisian simple stitch 2 together (Tss2tog): Insert hook through next 2 sts at same time, with hook remaining at front of work as for Tss. Yo, pull up lp—1 st decreased.

Tunisian full stitch (Tfs): Insert hook in space before next stitch, yo, pull up lp.

Poncho

First Panel

With A and Tunisian hook, ch 24.

Row 1: Tss in second ch from hook and each ch across—24 lps on hook. Return.

Row 2: Sk first vertical bar. *Tss2tog, yo. Repeat from * across to final st. Tss in last st—24 lps on hook. Return.

Row 3: Sk first vertical bar. *Tss in next vertical bar, Tfs in sp before next st. Repeat from * across to final st. Tss in last st—24 lps on hook. Return.

Repeat Rows 2–3 until panel measures approximately 15.5 in. (39.5 cm). Fasten off.

Second Panel

Using B, repeat first panel.

Border and Assembly

Join B in any corner of first panel. Using regular crochet hook, ch 1. Sc evenly around panel, working 2 or 3 sc in each corner to keep it square. Fasten off.

Repeat border on second panel with A. Weave in ends.

Arrange pieces so each panel folds over one shoulder. Make sure RS of each panel is on outside of poncho. Turn so WS is facing you. Sew seams where short side of one panel meets long side of other panel. Do not sew poncho closed on sides. Weave in ends. Lightly steam block on WS if desired.

6.5 in.
16.5 cm

5 in.
12.75 cm

seam

11 in.
28 cm

Poncho Panel

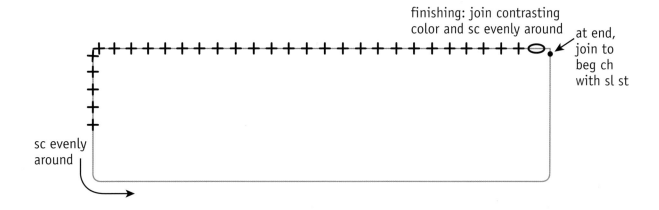

finishing: join contrasting color and sc evenly around at end, join to beg ch with sl st

sc evenly around

repeat Rows 2–3 until panel measures 15.5 in. (39.5 cm)

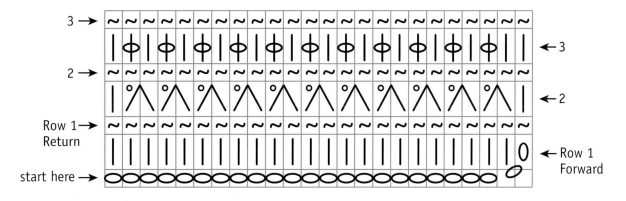

3 →
← 3
2 →
← 2
Row 1
Return
← Row 1
Forward
start here →

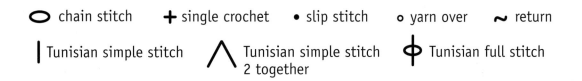

◯ chain stitch   ✚ single crochet   • slip stitch   ◦ yarn over   ~ return

| Tunisian simple stitch   ⋀ Tunisian simple stitch 2 together   ⏀ Tunisian full stitch

Turban

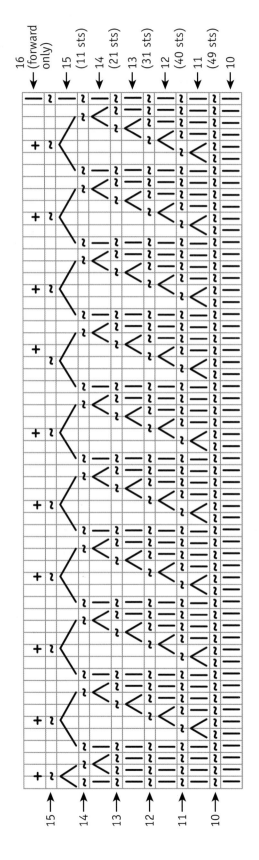

16
(forward only)
15
(11 sts)
14
(21 sts)
13
(31 sts)
12
(40 sts)
11
(49 sts)
10

15 →
14 →
13 →
12 →
11 →
10 →

repeat Rows 2–3 three times

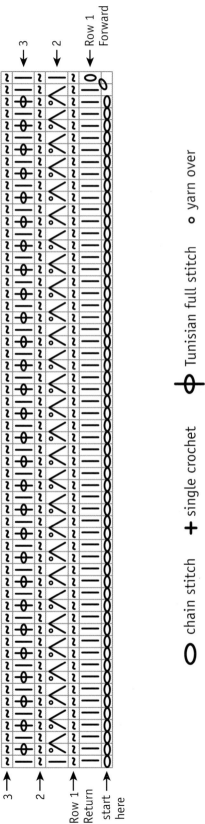

3
2
Row 1
Forward

3 →
2 →
Row 1 →
Return
start →
here

○ chain stitch   + single crochet   ⬍ Tunisian full stitch   o yarn over

| Tunisian simple stitch   ∧ Tunisian simple stitch 2 together   ʒ return

Row 1 →
Return
start →
here

Turban

With A and Tunisian crochet hook, ch 58.

Row 1: Tss in second ch from hook, and in each ch across—58 lps on hook. Return.

Row 2: Sk first vertical bar. *Tss2tog, yo. Repeat from * across to final st. Tss in last st—58 lps on hook. Return.

Row 3: Sk first vertical bar. *Tss in next vertical bar, Tfs in space before next st. Repeat from * across to final st. Tss in last st—58 lps on hook. Return.

Rows 4–9: Repeat Rows 2–3 three times.

Row 10: Sk first vertical bar. *Tss in next st. Repeat from * across—58 lps on hook. Return.

Row 11 (first decrease row): Sk first vertical bar. Tss in next 3 sts. *Tss2tog, Tss in next 4 sts. Repeat from * across—49 lps on hook. Return.

Row 12: Sk first vertical bar. Tss in next 2 sts. *Tss2tog, Tss in next 3 sts. Repeat from * until 1 st remains. Tss in last st—40 lps on hook. Return.

Row 13: Sk first vertical bar. Tss in next st. *Tss2tog, Tss in next 2 sts. Repeat from * until 2 sts remain. Tss in next 2 sts—31 lps on hook. Return.

Row 14: Sk first vertical bar. *Tss2tog, Tss in next st. Repeat from * across—21 lps on hook. Return.

Row 15: Sk first vertical bar. *Tss2tog. Repeat from * across—11 lps on hook. Return.

Row 16: Sk first vertical bar. Sc in each st across, inserting hook into each st as for Tss—10 sc. Fasten off.

Turban Trim

sc evenly around

join B at back seam

Brim

at end, join to beg ch with sl st

⬭ chain stitch   ✚ single crochet   • slip stitch

Trim and Finishing

With WS facing you, sew crown of hat closed. Sew back seam closed. Weave in ends.

With RS facing, join B at back seam. Using regular crochet hook, ch 1. Sc in each st around. Join to beg ch with sl st. Fasten off. Weave in ends.

Using a tapestry needle and B, pinch the front center of turban between bottom and fourth space above. Wind yarn around and through fabric approximately 10 times. Adjust bottom brim so trim shows. Tie yarn off securely on inside. Weave in ends.

Techniques

Traditional Crochet Skills Refresher

In traditional crochet—the style most people are familiar with—only one stitch at a time is active. Each is worked to completion before the next stitch is begun. Stitch heights progress from the low-profile slip stitch through single crochet, half double crochet, double crochet, treble crochet, and beyond, based on how many times the yarn is wrapped around the hook and how the loops are pulled through other loops. Hooks for traditional crochet are usually 5 to 8 in. (12.7 to 20.3 cm) long and can be made of metal, plastic, bamboo, wood, or other materials.

Chain Stitch (ch)

1. Attach yarn to hook with slip knot. Yarn over, pull through.

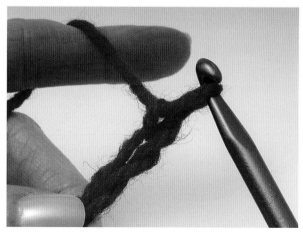

Slip Stitch (sl st)

1. Insert hook into work where instructed.
2. Yarn over, pull through both the stitch and the loop on the hook.

Single Crochet (sc)

1. Insert hook into work where instructed.
2. Yarn over, pull up a loop.

3. Yarn over, pull through both loops.

Half Double Crochet (hdc)

1. Yarn over.

2. Insert hook into work where instructed.
3. Yarn over, pull up a loop.

4. Yarn over, pull through all three loops.

Double Crochet (dc)

1. Yarn over.

2. Insert hook into the work where instructed.
3. Yarn over, pull up a loop.

4. Yarn over, pull through two loops.

5. Yarn over, pull through remaining two loops.

Treble Crochet (tr)

1. Yarn over twice.

2. Insert hook into the work where instructed.
3. Yarn over, pull up a loop.

4. Yarn over, pull through two loops.

5. Yarn over, pull through two loops.

6. Yarn over, pull through remaining two loops.

Change Colors or Start a New Yarn

1. Work the last stitch in the old color until two loops remain on hook, no matter what type of stitch it is.

2. Drop the current yarn to the back. Yarn over with the new color and complete the stitch.

3. Continue to work with new yarn.

Tunisian Crochet Skills Refresher

Tunisian crochet, also known as the "afghan stitch," combines aspects of crocheting and knitting. Like crocheting, it uses a hook and the same hand motions you are familiar with in traditional crochet; as in knitting, loops are added to the hook so there are many active stitches at once. Tunisian crochet uses either a long hook with a stopper on the end or a shorter hook with a plastic extension to accommodate the many loops that will be on the hook at one time. Tunisian fabric can look knitted, woven, or textured, and lacks the "loopy" appearance of traditional crochet.

Every Tunisian row is worked in two passes: the forward pass, which adds loops onto the hook, and the return pass, in which loops are worked off the hook. In the forward pass, you work various stitches as called for in the pattern. The return pass is always worked the same way regardless of the stitches used in the forward pass (except for special cases, such as shaping, where the pattern will specify a different return pass).

The photo shows a ChiaoGoo bamboo hook with a flexible extension and bead stopper.

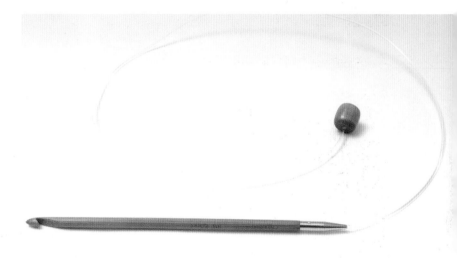

Here is a set of versatile Denise Interchangeable Crochet Hooks. Different size hooks can be attached to different lengths of plastic cord.

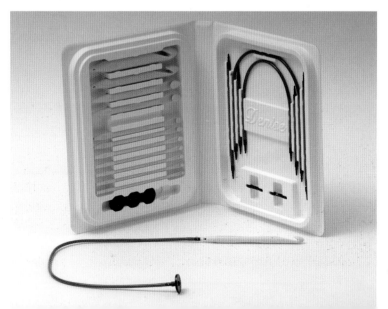

Tunisian Simple Stitch (Tss)

The instructions here are for working Tunisian simple stitch into a previous row of Tunisian crochet. You will also sometimes work Tunisian simple stitch into a foundation chain; the process is very similar.

To work into a previous row of Tunisian crochet: Look at the finished stitches. You will see a vertical bar for each stitch. These bars are what you will work behind as you make the Tunisian simple stitch forward pass.

1. Skip the first vertical bar that is on the far right side, directly below the hook. (Under the crocheter's thumb in the photo below.)

2. Put the hook from right to left through the next vertical bar. Keep the hook to the front of the work. Yarn over, pull up a loop. There will be two loops on the hook.

3. Repeat Step 2 in each stitch across, adding a loop to the hook with each stitch, until you get to the final vertical bar.

4. To work the final stitch, identify the final vertical bar and the horizontal thread that runs behind it. Insert the hook so it is behind both of these threads. When viewed from the side, the two threads look like a backwards 6 for right-handers and a regular 6 for lefties. Working the final stitch this way creates stability along the edge of the piece.

Yarn over, pull up a loop. Count the loops. You should have the same number as you did on the foundation row.

5. Return as described in the next section on the standard return.

The photo below shows Tunisian simple stitch fabric.

Standard Return

The return pass finishes the stitches of the forward pass and removes the loops from the hook. The photos show the standard return being worked in a row of Tunisian simple stitch worked into a foundation chain, but the return is worked exactly the same way no matter what stitches were worked in the forward pass. Unless the pattern specifies otherwise, you should always use this standard return pass.

1. Yarn over, pull through one loop.

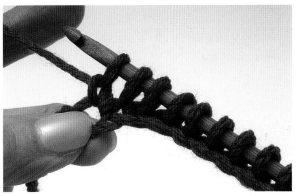

2. Yarn over, pull through two loops.

3. Repeat Step 2 all the way across until one loop remains on the hook.

Tunisian Knit Stitch (Tks)

To work Tunisian knit stitch into a previous row of Tunisian crochet, insert the hook through the center of each stitch from front to back. Look at the finished stitches. Each stitch has two "legs" in an upside-down V shape. You will work between these legs.

You can also work Tunisian knit stitch into a foundation chain. Because there are not previous stitches with horizontal bars or legs to work into, there is no difference between Tunisian knit stitch and Tunisian simple stitch when worked into the foundation chain.

1. Skip the first vertical bar that is on the far right side, directly below the hook.
2. Put the hook from front to back through the next stitch. You can stretch the stitch out slightly to see where the two vertical legs are; go right between them, not between two stitches. (The photos below show the hook inserted into the stitch from a front view and a back view.)

Yarn over. Pull up a loop. There will be two loops on the hook.

3. Repeat Step 2 in each stitch across (except for the far left bar), adding a loop to the hook with each stitch.

4. To work the final stitch, identify the final vertical bar and the horizontal thread that runs behind it. Insert the hook so it is behind both of these threads. When viewed from the side, the two threads look like a backwards 6 for right-handers and a regular 6 for lefties. Working the final stitch this way creates stability along the edge of the piece.

   Yarn over, pull up a loop. Count the loops. You should have the same number as you did on the foundation row.

5. Return as described for a standard return on page 115. The photo shows Tunisian knit stitch fabric.

Here is what it looks like on the back.

Tunisian Purl Stitch (Tps)

When working into a previous row of Tunisian crochet, you will insert the hook under the vertical bar of each stitch, just like for Tunisian simple stitch. The difference is that, in Tunisian purl stitch, the working yarn is held in front of the work. This creates the "purl bumps" in front of the stitches.

1. Skip the first vertical bar that is on the far right side, directly below the hook. Bring the yarn to the front of the work.

2. Insert the hook into the next vertical bar, keeping the hook to the front of the work. The photo shows the yarn being held in place by the right index finger.

3. Let the yarn go. Bring it toward you in front of the stitch, then back under the hook.

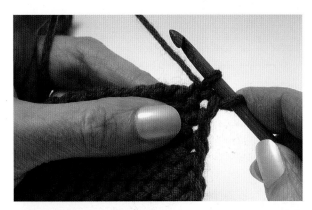

4. Yarn over, pull up a loop with that yarn. There will be two loops on the hook.

5. Repeat Steps 1–4 in each stitch across (except for the far left bar), adding a loop to the hook with each stitch. Notice the "purl bump" in the front of each stitch.

6. To work the final stitch, identify the final vertical bar and the horizontal thread that runs behind it. Leaving the yarn behind the work, insert the hook so it is behind both of these threads. When viewed from the side, the two threads look like a backwards 6 for right-handers and a regular 6 for lefties. Working the final stitch this way (as a Tunisian simple stitch instead of a Tunisian purl stitch) creates stability along the edge of the piece.

   Yarn over, pull up a loop. Count the loops. You should have the same number as you did on the foundation row.

7. Return as described for a standard return on page 115. The photo shows Tunisian purl fabric.

Working into the Foundation Chain

Working Tunisian stitches into the foundation chain is very similar to working them into a previous row of Tunisian fabric. The photos below show how to work Tunisian simple stitch or Tunisian knit stitch into a chain. Since there are no vertical bars in a chain, there is no difference in method or appearance between Tunisian simple stitch and Tunisian knit stitch worked into the chain.

1. Make the number of chain stitches indicated in the pattern.

   NOTE The number of Tunisian stitches on subsequent rows will be the same as the number of chains you start with.

2. Insert hook in second chain from hook. Yarn over, pull up loop. There will be two loops on the hook.

3. Insert the hook in the next chain. Yarn over, pull up loop.

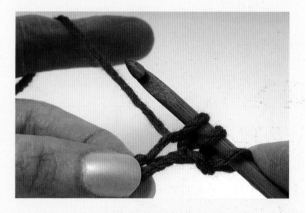

4. Continue in this fashion all the way across.

5. Count the loops. You should have the same number of loops on the hook as the number of foundation chains. If you are working evenly (without increasing or decreasing), remember this number, as this is the number of loops you should have at the end of every forward pass.

To work Tunisian purl stitch into a chain, insert the hook into the chain just as for Tunisian simple stitch (or Tunisian knit stitch), but with the yarn in front of the work. This creates the "purl bumps" in front of the stitches.

1. Bring the yarn to the front of the work.

2. Insert the hook into the second chain from the hook.

3. Let the yarn go. Bring it toward you in front of the stitch, then back under the hook.

4. Yarn over, pull up a loop with that yarn. There will be two loops on the hook.

5. Continue in this fashion all the way across, adding a loop to the hook with each stitch. Notice the "purl bump" in the front of each stitch. Follow the pattern instructions for whether the final stitch is a Tps or Tss.

Count the loops. You should have the same number of loops on the hook as the number of foundation chains. If you are working evenly (without increasing or decreasing), remember this number, as this is the number of loops you should have at the end of every forward pass.

Final Row

The top row of Tunisian crochet looks looser than the previous rows because nothing is worked into it. One way to end a piece neatly is to work single crochet stitches across the top of that row.

1. Insert your hook as you would for whatever stitch pattern you're using. In the example, this is Tunisian simple stitch.

2. Yarn over, pull up loop, yarn over, pull through two loops. This creates a single crochet.

3. Repeat Step 2 across.

Helpful Hints for Tunisian Crochet

- Never turn your work in Tunisian crochet. The right side is always facing you.

- Always skip the first vertical bar unless specifically instructed otherwise in the pattern.

- Pull the yarn snug at the start of each row to keep the edge from getting baggy.

- Work the final stitch on the forward pass into the vertical bar and the horizontal bar behind it for stability. If you turn that edge toward you, those two threads should look like a backwards 6 for right-handers and a regular 6 for lefties.

- You can work any stitch into any other type of stitch (for example, Tunisian purl stitch into Tunisian knit stitch, or Tunisian simple stitch into Tunisian purl stitch, and so on).

- Count! Check your stitch count regularly to make sure you did not miss picking up a stitch on a forward pass or mistakenly pull through the wrong number of loops on a return pass.

- To reduce the curl in Tunisian crochet, you can work the foundation row into the back bumps of the starting chains. Gently steam blocking your finished pieces will also help eliminate the curl.

Change Colors or Start a New Yarn

Sometimes you will need to change colors for a stripe pattern. You will also need to start a new ball of yarn when the previous one runs out. The method is the same in both cases.

The ideal place to start a new yarn is at the end of a return pass.

1. Work return pass until two loops remain on hook. Drop first yarn to the back. Yarn over with new yarn.

Pull through both loops.

Pull old and new tails firmly to hold stitches in place.

2. Continue working with the new yarn, making sure you are using the working end of the yarn and not the short tail.

Beyond the Basics

Here are some special techniques that add versatility to your repertoire once you have mastered the basics of regular and Tunisian crochet. Expand your skills with these shaping methods, textured stitch patterns, and embellishments, and learn how to use symbol charts to supplement the instructions in the written patterns.

Crochet Cast-On

The crochet cast-on can be used to add stitches at the end of a forward pass.

Rotate Tunisian hook so it points the opposite direction from usual (for right-handers, this will be to the right; for lefties, to the left).

NOTE The first CCO has two steps; each subsequent CCO requires only one step. Think of it like making ch sts on top of the hook.

First CCO: Bring yarn behind Tunisian hook. Insert a regular crochet hook from left to right in final st and under the Tunisian hook, yo, pull lp through. Move regular crochet hook to top of Tunisian hook, yo, pull lp through. Increase made.

Subsequent CCOs: Move yarn toward you then under and behind hook. Bring regular crochet hook in front of and on top of Tunisian hook. Yo, pull lp through. Increase made.

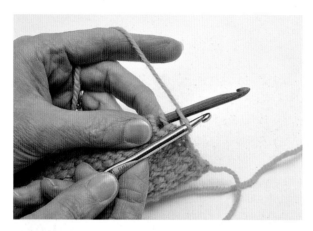

Final CCO: Slip last lp from regular crochet hook back onto Tunisian hook. Rotate Tunisian hook back into normal position and commence return pass.

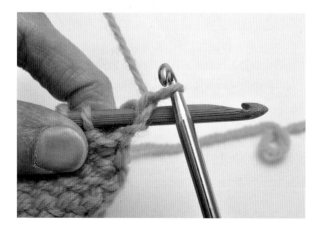

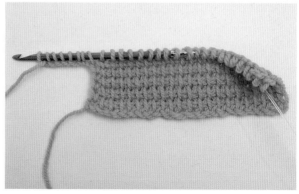

Loop Stitch (LS)

1. Insert hook into stitch as for sc.

2. Using a finger of your free hand, pull up the yarn to form a lp approximately 1 in. (2.5 cm) tall.

3. Put hook behind both both strands of the lp near the base and pull up both strands, leaving the loopy end sticking out the back.

4. Release lp from your finger. Using working yarn (not tall lp), yo, pull through all lps.

NOTE When loop stitch is worked correctly, the loops form on the back of the stitch.

Make 1 (M1)

Insert hook from front to back in space before next st.

Yo, pull up lp—1 st increased.

The photo below shows the completed M1 with a normal stitch worked afterward.

Marguerite Stitch
(worked into Tunisian crochet)

Row 1 (regular crochet): Ch 2. Insert hook in second ch from hook, yo, pull up lp.

Pull up lp in first vertical bar and in next 2 vertical bars (5 lps on hook).

Yo, pull through all 5 lps, ch 1.

*Insert hook in "eye" of flower just made, yo, pull up lp.

Pull up lp in last vertical bar of flower just made.

Pull up lp in next 2 vertical bars; yo, pull through all 5 lps on hook, ch 1.

Repeat from * across.

Tunisian cross stitch (X-st)

Sk next vertical bar, Tss in next vertical bar.

Now go back and locate the vertical bar that you skipped over (the one immediately before the one where you just made the Tss). The needle in the photo below marks this stitch.

Working in front of st just made, Tss in the skipped vertical bar.

A completed row of X-st.

Two rows X-st, two rows Tks, two rows X-st.

Tunisian Front Post Double Crochet (Tfpdc)

Yo.

Insert hook around both strands of vertical bar or around post, as indicated in pattern.

Yo, pull up lp.

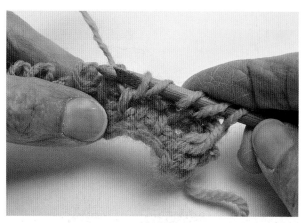

Yo, pull through 2 lps—1 lp added to hook.

Tunisian Knit Stitch 2 Together (Tks2tog)

Insert hook through next 2 sts at same time, with hook ending at back of work as for Tks.

Yo, pull up lp—1 st decreased.

How to Read Crochet Symbol Charts

Crochet instructions can be given in text or charts. A visual representation of a pattern can be very useful in understanding how the item is made.

Here are some guidelines for reading charts:
- Start by looking at the key to see which symbols represent which stitches. Make sure you know how to make the specified stitches.
- Patterns for crocheting in rows are charted row by row, starting with the foundation chain. Read the pattern starting at bottom left for the chain. In Tunisian crochet, each row is worked in two passes, shown in a row of boxes divided by a dotted or pale line. The forward pass is in the bottom two-thirds of each box and is read from right to left; the return pass is shown in the top third of each box and is read from left to right. The direction in which the chart is read corresponds to the direction in which you're actually working.
- In regular crochet sections, you will turn your work at the end of each row, which can make reading the charts a little confusing (on every other row, you will be working from right to left as always, but reading the line of the chart from left to right). Focus on working each new stitch into the stitch it is above in the chart.
- The loop on the hook at the beginning of every forward pass counts as a stitch and is represented in charts by a Tunisian simple stitch symbol. Do not work an additional stitch in that spot.
- When part of the pattern is repeated, this will be indicated in the chart to save space.
- Slanted lines can indicate shaping.

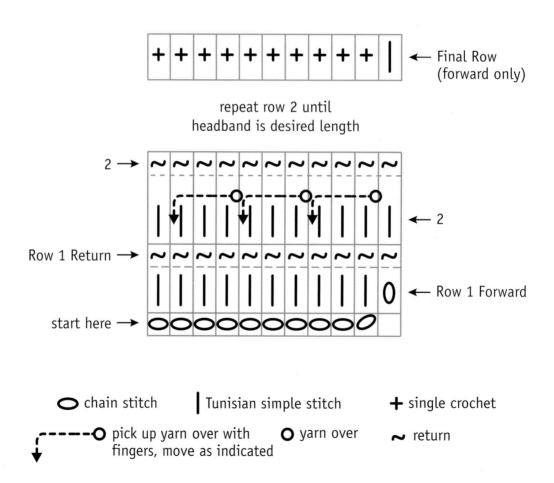

← Final Row (forward only)

repeat row 2 until headband is desired length

2 →   ← 2

Row 1 Return →   ← Row 1 Forward

start here →

⭕ chain stitch | Tunisian simple stitch   + single crochet

⊶O pick up yarn over with fingers, move as indicated   O yarn over   ~ return

Abbreviations

beg	beginning
CCO	crochet cast-on
ch, chs	chain, chains
dc	double crochet
dec	decrease
hdc	half double crochet
inc	increase
lp, lps	loop, loops
M1	make 1 (increase)
RS	right side
sc	single crochet
sc2tog	single crochet 2 together (decrease)
sk	skip
sl	slip
sl st	slip stitch
Tfpdc	Tunisian front post double crochet
Tfs	Tunisian full stitch
Tks	Tunisian knit stitch
Tks2tog	Tunisian knit stitch 2 together (decrease)
tog	together
Tps	Tunisian purl stitch
tr	treble crochet
Tss	Tunisian simple stitch
Tss2tog	Tunisian simple stitch 2 together (decrease)
X-st	Tunisian cross stitch
WS	wrong side
yo	yarn over

STANDARDS & GUIDELINES FOR CROCHET AND KNITTING

Standard Yarn Weight System

Categories of yarn, gauge ranges, and recommended needle and hook sizes

Yarn Weight Symbol & Category Names	(0) Lace	(1) Super Fine	(2) Fine	(3) Light	(4) Medium	(5) Bulky	(6) Super Bulky
Type of Yarns in Category	Fingering 10 count crochet thread	Sock, Fingering, Baby	Sport, Baby	DK, Light Worsted	Worsted, Afghan, Aran	Chunky, Craft, Rug	Bulky, Roving
Knit Gauge Range* in Stockinette Stitch to 4 inches	33 –40** sts	27–32 sts	23–26 sts	21–24 sts	16–20 sts	12–15 sts	6–11 sts
Recommended Needle in Metric Size Range	1.5–2.25 mm	2.25–3.25 mm	3.25–3.75 mm	3.75–4.5 mm	4.5–5.5 mm	5.5–8 mm	8 mm and larger
Recommended Needle U.S. Size Range	000 to 1	1 to 3	3 to 5	5 to 7	7 to 9	9 to 11	11 and larger
Crochet Gauge* Ranges in Single Crochet to 4 inch	32-42 double crochets**	21–32 sts	16–20 sts	12–17 sts	11–14 sts	8–11 sts	5–9 sts
Recommended Hook in Metric Size Range	Steel*** 1.6–1.4mm Regular hook 2.25 mm	2.25–3.5 mm	3.5–4.5 mm	4.5–5.5 mm	5.5–6.5 mm	6.5–9 mm	9 mm and larger
Recommended Hook U.S. Size Range	Steel*** 6, 7, 8 Regular hook B–1	B–1 to E–4	E–4 to 7	7 to I–9	I–9 to K–10½	K–10½ to M–13	M–13 and larger

* GUIDELINES ONLY: The above reflect the most commonly used gauges and needle or hook sizes for specific yarn categories.

** Lace weight yarns are usually knitted or crocheted on larger needles and hooks to create lacy, openwork patterns. Accordingly, a gauge range is difficult to determine. Always follow the gauge stated in your pattern.

*** Steel crochet hooks are sized differently from regular hooks--the higher the number, the smaller the hook, which is the reverse of regular hook sizing.

This Standards & Guidelines booklet and downloadable symbol artwork are available at: **YarnStandards.com**

SKILL LEVELS FOR CROCHET

1 ◖□□□▢ **Beginner** — Projects for first-time crocheters using basic stitches. Minimal shaping.

2 ◖■□□▢ **Easy** — Projects using yarn with basic stitches, repetitive stitch patterns, simple color changes, and simple shaping and finishing.

3 ◖■■□▢ **Intermediate** — Projects using a variety of techniques, such as basic lace patterns or color patterns, mid-level shaping and finishing.

4 ◖■■■▶ **Experienced** — Projects with intricate stitch patterns, techniques and dimension, such as non-repeating patterns, multicolor techniques, fine threads, small hooks, detailed shaping and refined finishing.

This Standards & Guidelines booklet and downloadable symbol artwork are available at: **YarnStandards.com**

Head Circumference Chart

	Infant/Child				Adult	
	Premie	**Baby**	**Toddler**	**Child**	**Woman**	**Man**
Circumference						
(in.)	12	14	16	18	20	22
(cm.)	30.5	35.5	40.5	45.5	50.5	56

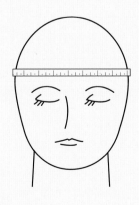

For an accurate head measure, place a tape measure across the forehead and measure around the full circumference of the head. Keep the tape snug for accurate results.

Baby's size	3 months	6 months	12 months	18 months	24 months
1. Chest (in.)	16	17	18	19	20
(cm.)	40.5	43	45.5	48	50.5
2. Center Back	10½	11½	12½	14	18
Neck-to-Cuff	26.5	29	31.5	35.5	45.5
3. Back Waist	6	7	7½	8	8½
Length	15.5	17.5	19	20.5	21.5
4. Cross Back	7¼	7¾	8¼	8½	8¾
(Shoulder to	18.5	19.5	21	21.5	22
shoulder)					
5. Sleeve Length	6	6½	7½	8	8½
to Underarm	15.5	16.5	19	20.5	21.5

Child's size	2	4	6	8	10
1. Chest (in.)	21	23	25	26½	28
(cm.)	53	58.5	63.5	67	71
2. Center Back	18	19½	20½	22	24
Neck-to-Cuff	45.5	49.5	52	56	61
3. Back Waist	8½	9½	10½	12½	14
Length	21.5	24	26.5	31.5	35.5
4. Cross Back	9¼	9¾	10¼	10¾	11¼
(Shoulder to	23.5	25	26	27	28.5
shoulder)					
5. Sleeve Length	8½	10½	11½	12½	13½
to Underarm	21.5	26.5	29	31.5	34.5

Books

Association of Japan Knit Culture. *100 Tunisian Crochet Patterns (Japanese)*. Japan: Nihon Vogue-Sha Co. Ltd., 2007.

Barnden, Betty. *The Crochet Stitch Bible*. Iola, WI: Krause Publications, 2004.

Christmas, Carolyn and Dorris Brooks. *101 Easy Tunisian Stitches*. Berne, IN: Annie's Attic, 2004.

Guzman, Kim. *Tunisian Crochet Stitch Guide*. Little Rock, AR: Leisure Arts, Inc., 2013.

Guzman, Kim. *Ultimate Beginner's Guide to Tunisian Crochet*. Little Rock, AR: Leisure Arts, Inc., 2012.

Matthews, Anne. *Vogue Dictionary of Crochet Stitches*. Newton, UK: David & Charles, 1987.

Ohrenstein, Dora. *The New Tunisian Crochet*. Loveland, CO: Interweave Press LLC, 2012.

Reader's Digest. *The Ultimate Sourcebook of Knitting and Crochet Stitches*. Pleasantville, NY: Reader's Digest, 2003.

Silverman, Sharon Hernes. *Crochet Pillows*. Mechanicsburg, PA: Stackpole Books, 2011.

Silverman, Sharon Hernes. *Crochet Scarves*. Mechanicsburg, PA: Stackpole Books, 2012.

Silverman, Sharon Hernes. *Tunisian Crochet*. Mechanicsburg, PA: Stackpole Books, 2009.

Yarn

Crystal Palace Yarns
www.straw.com

Lily
www.sugarncream.com

Lion Brand Yarn Company
www.lionbrand.com

Muench Yarns
www.muenchyarns.com

Plymouth Yarn Company, Inc.
www.plymouthyarn.com

Tahki Stacy Charles, Inc.
www.tahkistacycharles.com

Hooks

ChiaoGoo/Westing Bridge LLC
www.chiaogoo.com

Denise Interchangeable Knitting and Crochet
www.knitdenise.com

Stitch Diva Studios
www.stitchdiva.com

Other Crochet Resources

Craft Yarn Council of America (CYCA)
The craft yarn industry's trade association has educational links, information on standards for yarn and hooks, and free projects.
www.craftyarncouncil.com

Crochet Guild of America (CGOA)
The national association for crocheters, CGOA sponsors conventions, offers correspondence courses, and maintains a membership directory.
www.crochet.org

The National NeedleArts Association (TNNA)
This international trade organization represents retailers, manufacturers, distributors, designers, manufacturers' representatives, publishers, teachers, and wholesalers of products and supplies for the specialty needlearts market.
www.tnna.org

Ravelry
This free online community for knitters, crocheters, and other fiber fans is the place to exchange information, manage projects, get advice on techniques, and keep up with everything yarn related.
www.ravelry.com

Yahoo
You can see projects, ask questions, share photos, and learn about all things related to Tunisian crochet by joining the Tunisian Crochet group on Yahoo.
http://groups.yahoo.com/neo/groups/tunisiancrochet/info

Acknowledgments

Thanks to everyone who helped this book become a reality. I am grateful to those who provided supplies: Susan C. Druding, Cathy Campbell, and Andrea Gaeta of Crystal Palace Yarns; Stacy Charles and Melody Desola of Tahki Stacy Charles, Inc.; Brandyce Pechillo of Lion Brand Yarn Company; Kirstin B. Muench of Muench Yarns, Inc.; and Cia Abbott Bullemer of Plymouth Yarn Company, Inc.

The cover photograph was taken by Tiffany Blackstone, with the essential cooperation of her beautiful baby. Thank you as always to photographer Alan Wycheck for his collaboration and indispensible visual contributions to this, our sixth book together. Location styling was accomplished with the expert help of Doreen Gadel. Many thanks to our very accommodating models Domenic Scarcia and Parker Lapiska and their helpful and enthusiastic parents, Tara and Nicholas Scarcia and Kelly and Justin Lapiska.

Many thanks to Mark Allison, Editor; Kathryn Fulton, Associate Editor; Candi Derr, Assistant Editor; and Judith M. Schnell, Publisher and Vice President of Stackpole Books. The book's design, cover, and symbol charts are due to the time and meticulous effort of Caroline Stover. Heather Gooch brought energy and experience to the marketing phase of the project.

Thanks to the Craft Yarn Council of America for permission to reprint standards, to the Crochet Guild of America (CGOA) for industry information and news, and to The National NeedleArts Association (TNNA) for its support of yarn industry professionals.

Three cheers for my inspiring colleagues in the world of crochet design! Our interaction has been valuable and enjoyable, and I look forward to spending more time with you.

As always, my deepest gratitude goes to my friends and family, especially my husband, Alan, and our sons, Jason and Steven.

Visual Index

Checkerboard Blanket 2

Checkerboard Hat 6

Honeycomb Pullover 10

Sherbet Stripes Blanket 18

Sherbet Stripes Hat 22

Infant Cocoon and Hat 27

Christening Gown 34

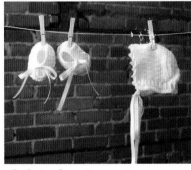

Christening Bonnet and Booties 34

Strappy Pants 53

Sunny Bow Headband 58

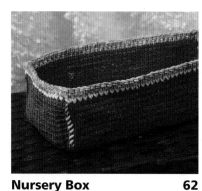

Nursery Box 62

Washcloth Quartet 65

Harlequin Blanket 73

Thumbless Mittens 79

Zippered Hoodie 82

Favorite Skirt 97

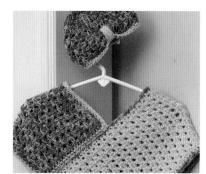

**Spring Poncho
and Turban** 101